Understanding Arabs

The InterAct Series
Edited by
GEORGE W. RENWICK

Other books in the Series
AUSTRALIA/U.S.
A COMMON CORE: THAIS AND AMERICANS
WITH RESPECT TO THE JAPANESE
GOOD NEIGHBORS: COMMUNICATING WITH THE MEXICANS

Understanding Arabs

A GUIDE FOR WESTERNERS

MARGARET K. NYDELL

INTERCULTURAL PRESS INC.
YARMOUTH, MAINE

To my parents, Leo and Helen Kleffner

Printed in the United States of America

Library of Congress Cataloging-in-Publication Data

Nydell, Margaret K. (Margaret Kleffner)
    Understanding Arabs.

    (The InterAct series)
    Bibliography: p.
    1. Arabs.   I. Title.   II. Series.
DS36.77.N93   1987   909ʹ.04927   86-83102
ISBN 0-933662-65-3 (pbk.)

Contents

Map of the Arab World *vi*

Preface *vii*

Introduction: Patterns of Change 1

1. Beliefs and Values 15
2. Friends and Strangers 19
3. Emotion and Logic 33
4. Getting Personal 41
5. Men and Women 51
6. Social Formalities and Etiquette 57
7. The Social Structure 69
8. The Role of The Family 75
9. Religion and Society 87
10. Communicating with Arabs 99

    Conclusion 111

    Appendix A. The Arabic Language 113

    Appendix B. The Arab Countries:

            Similarities and Differences 123

Notes *149*

Bibliography and References *157*

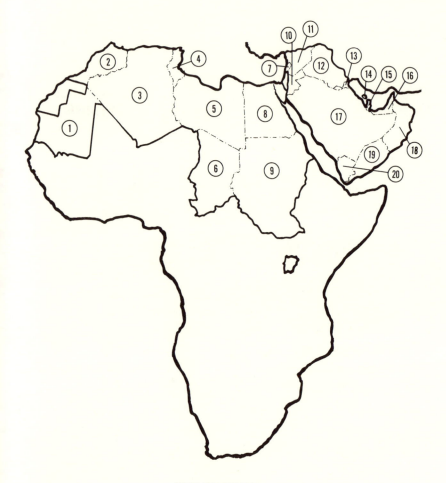

THE ARAB WORLD

1. Mauritania
2. Morocco
3. Algeria
4. Tunisia
5. Libya

6. Chad
7. Lebanon
8. Egypt
9. Sudan
10. Jordan

11. Syria
12. Iraq
13. Kuwait
14. Bahrain
15. Qatar

16. United Arab Emirates
17. Saudi Arabia
18. Oman
19. Yemen, PDR
20. Yemen Arab Republic

Preface

The purpose of this book is to provide a cross-cultural guide for foreigners who are living in an Arab country, who encounter Arabs frequently, or who are interested in the behavior of Arabs, whether encountered in the media or personally. It is written particularly for Westerners—North Americans and Europeans—and underlines the contrasts between Western and Arab societies. It is for non-specialists who want or need to have a clearer understanding of the thought patterns, social relationships, and ways of life of modern Arabs.

Most of us are aware of the degree to which different national and cultural groups stereotype each other, even in person-to-person relations. When Westerners and Arabs interact, especially if neither group understands the other, they often come away with impressions which are *mutually negative*.

It is my hope that this book will help alleviate that problem in two ways: (1) by explaining some of the behavioral characteristics of Arabs in terms of cultural background, thereby deepening the reader's understanding and helping to avoid negative interpretations; and (2) serving as a guide to cross-cultural interaction with Arabs which will help people avoid inadvertent insults and errors of etiquette.

Foreigners find very little material available to help them understand Arab society. Not much has been written on the subject of Arab cultural and social practices, either in Arabic or in English. A great deal of the material which exists is over twenty years old and sounds dated to anyone who is familiar with Arab society today. Observations made only ten years ago are often no longer applicable. In recent years changes taking place in education, housing, health, technology and other areas have also caused marked changes in attitudes and customs.

The most serious deficiency in research about Arab society is the lack of attention given to modern, urban, and often Western-educated Arabs. Researchers, especially anthropologists, have tended to focus on village life and nomadic groups and to study traditional social patterns. Interesting as these studies are, they offer little directly-applicable information for Westerners who will, for the most part, observe or interact with Arabs who are well-educated, well-traveled, and often very sophisticated.

This book is an attempt to fill that gap. It focuses on the socially elite—businessmen, bureaucrats, managers, scientists, professors, and intellectuals—and the ways in which they interact with foreigners and with each other. In most Arab countries, the elite differ considerably from rural or tradition-oriented social groups; indeed, some types of behavior which are required by the norms of one group are considered obsolete by another. At the same time, many basic traditions and customs still determine the way of life of all Arabs and affect their goals, values, and codes of accepted behavior. The many similarities among social groups and among the various Arab countries still outweigh their differences so that valid generalizations are possible. Any significant differences among groups will be pointed out.

It is important that Westerners who interact with upper-class, educated Arabs be aware of the particular characteristics of Arab etiquette and patterns of behavior and thought, since the differences may be quite subtle and, initially, hard to identify. It is easy to be lulled into the security of assuming that the superficial similarities of appearance, dress, and life-style among educated Arabs mean that they are "just like us." One is more likely to remain alert for differing social proprieties when seated in a tent or a mud-floored village house; it is not so easy to remember the differences when seated in the living room of a modern home, surrounded by Western-style furnishings and English-speaking Arabs.

I realize that any attempt to describe the motives and values of an entire people is risky since, on the one hand, it leads to generalizations which are not true in all cases and, on the other, it necessarily involves the observer's perspectives and interpretations and leads to emphasizing some traits over others. I have tried to present a balanced view, one which is generally descriptive of Arabs throughout the entire cultural area of the "Arab World." Most of the material in this book comes from my own personal experiences and from interviews with others over a period of 20 years. These interviews have taken place in virtually all of the Arab countries—in North Africa, the Levant, the Fertile Crescent, and the Arabian Peninsula.

It would be tempting simply to list all the charming, attractive, admirable qualities found in Arab society and let it go at that, but this is not a book written for tourist agencies. That kind of information, while interesting, is generally of little practical value to a person who must live in Arab society and/or interact with Arabs on a regular basis about substantive matters. To be of real value in helping people deal with cross-cultural relationships in the Arab World, we must look at as many differences as possible and focus especially on "problem areas," not on the delightful surprises awaiting the foreigner (the wonderful food, the kindness to children and elderly people, the lack of violent crime). It is these problem areas which need our attention, study, and thought; to leave them out would be to shortchange the reader.

To my knowledge, no book like this has ever been written by an Arab with the intention of introducing Western people and social patterns to the Arabs. Such a book would be welcome indeed!

The Arabs have been subjected to so much direct or indirect criticism by the West that they are very sensitive to a Westerner's statements about them. I have made an effort to be fair and honest and, at the same time, sympathetic to the Arab way of life, especially when contrasting Arab and Western cultural behavior. I have described differences while trying to avoid value judgments; there is no assumption that one cultural approach is superior to the other.

Note: The Arabic words which appear in this book are not written in detailed phonemic transcription. They are spelled with conventional English letters and are an approximation of the way the words should be pronounced.

I owe thanks to many people whose insights and stories contributed to this book. To all the students, diplomats, and businessmen with whom I spent hours discussing cultural and social experiences, this is a word of thanks to you as a group.

In particular I thank my husband, Carl, for his assistance in all phases of preparation of this book. Parts of the manuscript were read by Les Benedict, Helen Edwards, John McCaffrey, Mary Joy McGregor and Janet Schoenike, all of whom offered valuable comments and suggestions. I also thank Dr. George Selim of the Library of Congress and Dr. Mahmoud Esmail Sieny of King Saud University for their assistance.

Most of all, I thank the Arabs. My experiences with them over the years have added much pleasure and richness to my life.

MARGARET K. NYDELL

Understanding Arabs

Introduction: Patterns of Change

Arab society has been subjected to enormous pressures from the outside world, particularly since the Second World War. Social change is already evident because the effects of economic modernization have been felt in every area of life. Even for nomads and residents of remote villages the traditional way of life is disappearing.

Westernization

Most social changes have come through the adoption of Western technology, health care systems, educational concepts and political ideas. Westernization is controversial but inevitable; it is an on-going process and is present to varying degrees in all of the Arab countries.

The Arab countries have experienced an influx of foreign advisors, managers, businessmen, teachers, engineers, health care personnel, politicians, and tourists. Through personal contacts and increased media exposure, Arabs are learning how "outsiders" live. Thousands of Arab students have been educated in the West and returned with changed attitudes, even changed personalities.

Arab governments are building schools, hospitals, housing

units, and industrial complexes so fast that entire cities and towns change their appearance in a few years. It is easy to feel lost in some Arab cities if you have been away only a year or two. Modern hotels are found in any large Arab city, the streets and roads are full of cars, and the telephone, telex, and airline services are often overtaxed. Imported consumer products are abundant in most Arab countries, ranging from white wedding dresses to supermarkets. While these are surface changes, they symbolize deeper shifts in values.

In the last twenty years the number of educated people has doubled in some Arab countries and increased ten times or more in others. Over-all levels of literacy have increased from below 10% to 50-70% in the Arabian Peninsula and show an equally dramatic increase among rural people in most Arab countries. Saudi Arabia is opening schools at the rate of more than one a day; its five-year plan för 1975-1980 projected a nearly doubled enrollment in primary schools during that time alone, from 600,000 to one million students.[1] Jordan had 25 religious schools in 1921; in 1977 it had 2,400 public schools and nearly a third of its population were involved in education, as teachers or as students at home or abroad.[2] In Iraq the number of students in primary schools increased 101% between 1968 and 1978.[3] Similarly, the number of primary school students doubled in Sudan between 1969 and 1976, and the number of teachers tripled.[4] In Kuwait there were 3,600 students in 1945 (at all levels), 45,000 in 1960, and 250,000 in 1975.[5]

Education at the university level is growing even faster; university education is free in most Arab countries, and students studying abroad receive stipends from their governments. Saudi university students increased from 12,000 to 31,000 between 1975 and 1980; this included nearly 11,000 studying abroad, compared with fewer than 2,000 in 1971.[6] In Sudan the government announced a plan to triple the number of university students between 1977 and 1983.[7] Egypt, with a population of about 42 million, has one million students enrolled in universities.[8]

More Arab women are becoming educated and active professionally. The number of women in the non-agricultural work sector in 1975 was approximately 15% in Egypt and Sudan, 20% in Syria and Yemen, and over 20% in Lebanon.[9] This percentage will increase dramatically as educational programs for girls and young women are expanded. In all Arab countries the percentage of girls in the total student population is increasing steadily and nearing the 50% mark. In Kuwait girls comprised only 5% of the student enrollment in 1945, but increased to 30% by 1965 and 45% in 1975.[10] In Saudi Arabia the education of girls began in 1956, and the enrollment of female students rose from virtually none to nearly 300,000 in 1974.[11] By 1980 almost all girls were enrolled, and in 1983 the Saudi government announced that more than 2,000 more girls' schools were under construction.[12]

Improved health care is changing the quality and length of life. In Jordan the number of physicians increased by more than 40% between 1971 and 1977, the number of dentists doubled, and the number of pharmacists more than doubled.[13] Oman has more hospitals today than it had hospital beds in 1970.[14] The number of hospital beds in Saudi Arabia rose from 4,000 in 1975 to 11,400 in 1980.[15]

Life expectancy in the Arab countries has risen very quickly as health programs improve. Between 1955 and 1978 life expectancy went from 43 to 53 years of age in Morocco and Algeria, from 42 to 54 in Egypt, from 34 to 45 in Saudi Arabia, and from 55 to 69 in Kuwait.[16] Population statistics show an average growth rate of 3% or more between 1975 and 1980 in almost all Arab countries; those in the Arabian Gulf increased by as much as 7%.[17]

All over the Arab World, the population is shifting from farms and villages to large urban centers, and nomads are changing to a sedentary life. Urbanization is increasing in virtually every Arab country; the amount of increase between 1950 and 1970 may be seen in the following table:

Percentage of Urbanization[18]		
	1950	1970
Morocco	23	35
Algeria	25	35
Tunisia	31	45
Libya	22	38
Egypt	32	45
Syria	35	43
Lebanon	40	58
Jordan	35	44
Kuwait	51	80
Qatar	50	70
Saudi Arabia	9	25

In 1980 urbanization had risen to 40-60% in Algeria, Tunisia, Egypt, Syria, Lebanon, and Jordan.[19]

In a survey of 1,600 Bedouin families conducted in Jordan in 1978, almost 95% lived not in tents but in houses of stone, concrete, or sun-dried clay. Many of the men were engaged in sedentary occupations or working for the army or the government. The researchers reported:

> Most parents admitted that the way of life they knew was not what they wanted for their children. . . . The University researchers found that there was a general willingness among the Bedouin to settle down permanently.[20]

Some of the other major social changes and trends in the Arab World are listed below:

–Family planning is promoted in most Arab countries and is increasingly practiced. This is accepted as permissible practice by most Islamic jurists.[21]

–People have far more exposure to newspapers, television and radio.

–People are choosing more entertainment outside the home and family.

–More people travel and study abroad.

–Parents are finding that they have less control over their children's choice of career and lifestyle.

–More people are working for large, impersonal organizations and industries.

–Business organizations are becoming increasingly involved in international trade.

–There has been a significant increase in political awareness and participation.

–Arab governments are promoting the idea of national identity to replace regional or kin-group loyalty.

The issue for Arabs is not whether they want Westernization and modernization—the momentum cannot be stopped now. They must find ways of adopting modern concepts with minimal disruption to the traditions they value.

The Effects of Change

The disruptive effects of the sudden introduction of foreign practices and concepts on traditional societies are well known, and the Arabs have not been spared. The social strains among groups of people who represent different levels of education and Western exposure can be intense. In Arab society these mutual frustrations exist to a degree which can hardly be imagined by Westerners.

Many younger Arabs admire and even prefer Western dress, entertainment and "liberal" thought, to the distress of older or more traditional Arabs. The "generation gap" is widening in the Arab World, excruciatingly painful in some communities and families. A Westernized Arab once equated the feelings of an Arab father whose son refuses to accept the family's choice of a bride with the feelings of a Western father who discovers that his son is on drugs.

Arab writers and journalists frequently address the theme of the necessity for scrutinizing Western innovations, adopting those aspects which are beneficial to their society (such as scientific and technical knowledge) and rejecting those which are harmful, such as a lessening concern for family cohesion, or entertainment involving the consumption of alcohol. A representative passage is found in Dr. Algosaibi's essay, "Arabs and Western civilization":

> To sum up: we must not take an attitude to the West based on sentiment, emotion or fanaticism. We must scrutinize the elements of Western civilization carefully, and in doing so learn from its sciences and identify in its intellectual heritage those areas which we may need to adopt or acquire. At the same time, we must recognize its callous traits so that we may repudiate them out of hand. Perhaps in such a balanced view there will be something that will help us to build anew in our land a new and vital Arab way of life comparable to that ancient civilization of ours which once led the whole world.[22]

Arnold Hottinger has described the dilemma that the pressures to modernize impose on Arabs:

> . . . the passage [toward modernization] cannot be accomplished calmly and in unison—with gradual changes in intellectual outlook, the spontaneous growth and spread of new ideas, and generational evolution. No, there is always something forced about it. One is driven to act by material, economic, and military necessities, by the very need for national survival—although it should be a part of realistic politics to provide a certain shelter against those pressures, in order to provide elbowroom for the complex process of mental and economic evolution. Instead of generating change from the inside, one is often forced to take much of it over from the outside, by imitating an outside world which is felt—not without reason—to be alien and menacing. In short, one must learn from that world, even imitate it, in order

to defend oneself against it, with the ultimate aim of remaining oneself.[23]

There is a "dualism" present in modern Arab society, where both modernist and traditionalist ways of thinking are present at the same time. Abdallah Laroui has described the dualism in educational institutions—on the one hand, there are scientific, technological and commercial institutes which prepare students for service in the modern sector and offer (often in a foreign language) the most advanced programs and methods; on the other hand, there are educational institutes (teaching humanities, law, or theology) which either remain rigidly faithful to traditional practices or dedicate themselves to maintaining traditional values in the face of changing practices. He concludes that traditionalist thought still dominates:

> Traditionalist thought therefore, be it predominantly religious or predominantly cultural, reigns everywhere. From these [latter] establishments come the intellectual elite (teachers, writers, journalists, preachers, etc.), and the greater part of the political elite (members of the parliaments, of the parties, of numerous committees, etc.). By its very existence this generalized duality guarantees the perpetuity of traditionalist thought, for it both knowingly maintains the preponderance of the traditional sector and allows the petite bourgeoisie to preserve the leading role in the domains of politics and culture.[24]

There has been much discussion about the subject of adapting modern educational concepts and needs to Islamic values. The outlook and concerns of Moslem educators are well represented by the following passages written by participants in the first World Conference in Muslim Education, held in Mecca in 1977:

> Education has been the most effective method of changing the attitudes of the young and thus leading them to accept and initiate social change. Modern Western education places an exaggerated emphasis upon reason and rationality and underestimates the value of the spirit. It encourages scientific enquiry at the

expense of faith; it promotes individualism; it breeds scepticism; it refuses to accept that which is not demonstrable; it is anthropocentric rather than theocentric. Even where it does not directly challenge faith, it relegates it to the background as something much less important than reason.[25]

. . . a chasm has been created between "traditional" and "modern" society. . . . The Muslim world did not have time to think over the complexities that it was courting.[26]

The content of education . . . can be divided for a Muslim into two categories: experience in the form of skills or technical knowledge whose nature varies from age to age and which is bound to change constantly; and experience based on certain constant or permanent values embodied in religion and scripture. . . . Believing as it does that the true aim of education is to produce men who have faith as well as knowledge, the one sustaining the other, Islam does not think that the pursuit of knowledge by itself without reference to the spiritual goal that man must try to attain, can do humanity much good. Knowledge divorced from faith is not only partial knowledge, it can even be described as a kind of new ignorance.[27]

The spirit of Islam should, therefore, be the dominant feature in all text-books on whatever subject. Moreover, all our courses, books, and teaching materials should have as their central theme the relationship between God, Man and the Universe.[28]

In the Islamic educational system, textbooks should be prepared so that they reflect the Islamic outlook even as they present the pertinent "modern" theories and discoveries. One educator suggested, for example, that, in the natural sciences, the word "Nature" be replaced with the word "Allah" so that it is clear that God is the source of natural growth and development, the properties of chemicals, the laws of physics and astronomy, and the like. Historical events would be evaluated not for military or political significance but by their success in furthering the spiritual aims of mankind—for example, an agnostic society which amassed a great empire would not be judged as "successful."[29]

The "outside" pressure toward change is certainly visible

physically as one looks at the changes in Arab cities and housing. This is well described by Thomas and Deakin:

The conservative monarchs or radical presidents might try to stem the tide and restrain alien influences, but there is a feeling at times that, in general, the Arab is parting company with his own culture. Perhaps the most obvious visual example of this is the obliteration of an architectural tradition. The modern skyscrapers of central Beirut are symptomatic of the sheer physical intrusion of much modern building in the Arab World. In Jidda in Saudi Arabia, glass and concrete offices and hotels which have to be kept alive by whole banks of air-conditioners are sprouting above the ruins of exquisite thick-walled houses designed over centuries of trial and error to "condition" themselves. The heart of Damascus, a city already ancient in biblical times, has recently been torn out and replaced by rectangular conformity.[30]

Most Arabs who are well educated and engaged in professional work have learned to balance the demands of modern life with traditional values and concerns. Arab women may be doctors or scientists, but they still acknowledge their place in the family structure and believe in the need to guard their reputation carefully.

In researching the personality of Saudi college students, Dr. Levon Melikian quoted one student as saying:

I am several persons at the same time. I am both progressive and reactionary, happy and unhappy, religious and secularly minded, conservative and liberal, backward-looking and forward-looking.[31]

President Anwar Sadat could easily leave the affairs of state to spend time in his home village, where he donned a long white robe and sat discussing crops and local events with his boyhood friends. Sadat expressed his feelings about his village in his book, *In Search of Identity:*

This was not all I came to learn in Mit Abul-Kum. For I learned something else that has remained with me all my life: the fact that wherever I go, wherever I happen to be, I shall always know where I really am. I can never lose my way because I know that I have living roots there, deep down in the soil of my village, in that land out of which I grew, like the trees and the plants.[32]

Westerners see a dual personality present in many educated Arabs who have the ability to synthesize two diverse ways of thinking and appreciate both. This is well illustrated by tracing the history of one man and his children.

Salim Osman was born in 1890 in a small village near Cairo. When I met him as an old man, he happily recounted the two incidents in his childhood which he most vividly remembered. When he was very small, his hand was bitten through the palm by a camel and severed nearly in two. The Bedouin owner prescribed the then best-known cure: bathing his hand in hot oil and wrapping it in gauze. The hand healed so well that he regained full use of it. The other story concerned his marriage ceremony at age 15 when, by arrangement, he married a woman of 20. In other words, Salim Osman spent his youth embedded in the ancient traditions of the Arab World.

By the time he was eighteen, Salim had three daughters. He was a moderately prosperous farmer but felt stifled by village life. He ran off to Cairo, enrolled in the Azhar University, and obtained a degree in Arabic language studies. He found work in the city as a tutor and continued to enlarge his reputation to the point where he was finally appointed to teach the young King Farouk. In the heady social atmosphere of palace life, he met a Turkish noblewoman. He divorced his first wife, married the lady, and had three more children; ten years later they were divorced. His third marriage was brief and childless. When Salim was in his late forties, he married his last wife, the 18-year-old daughter of a friend, by whom he had five more children.

After the Egyptian revolution in 1952, Salim joined the government's Ministry of Education and retired in 1960 as a director of teachers' institutes. He read widely and was known for his wisdom and piety. He was particularly interested in space exploration and modern medicine and considered the achievements in both areas as "miracles from God."

Salim encouraged his children, both sons and daughters, to further their education and lived to see one son study in England and one in the U.S. His two oldest daughters remained in the village, married farmers and lived in homes of mud-straw brick. His two youngest daughters are professionals—one is a lawyer and one a chemical engineer. One son became a general in the army, and one a university professor of economics.

Salim died in 1968, the patriarch of his large and diverse family. He is buried in the ancient graveyard of his village, in a traditional tomb of whitewashed brick. His grave is visited annually by all of his children.

Fundamentalism

Young Arabs are generally well educated, and they find themselves torn, even more than their parents were, between different sets of values. Most of them try to find a compromise. Some, however, view Western influences as ominous and threatening and feel that they should be rejected entirely.

In the last ten years, the most noticeable reaction to the threat of Westernization has consisted of religious revivals such as "Islamic fundamentalism" (called by some, and perhaps more accurately, "Islamic consciousness"). For an Arab who cherishes his traditions and feels that his identity is jeopardized, fundamentalist Islam is something he can cling to. The Islamic religion is the only aspect of the modern Arab World that has not been, and cannot be, affected by Westernization.

The result has been a marked increase in traditional activities and in the use of symbolic gestures which reconfirm the old Arab and Islamic values. Some women are once again wearing floor-length, long-sleeved dresses and covering their hair; religious studies have increased in universities; the publication of religious tracts has increased; more religious orations are heard in public. The number of religious broadcasts and of Islamic newspapers and books has tripled in the last decade.[33]

In Arab politics, there has been a resurrection of the term "Jihad" ("Holy War") and an emphasis on Islamic brotherhood and unity. A notable example is the Pan-Islamic movement, begun in 1969 by King Faisal of Saudi Arabia, which has led to several Islamic summit conferences and aims at achieving greater political unity among Moslem nations. Some Arab governments have found themselves severely criticized and even openly challenged if they are viewed as too liberal or too cooperative with the West.

It is not surprising that the sentiments of some groups are increasingly anti-Western and that statements and actions are directed against Western governments, cultural symbols, and even individuals. Many social ills are blamed wrongly on the influence of Westernization, but some of the blame is surely justified.

In his book *Science, Technology, and Development in the Muslim World,* Sardar quotes a passage from the prospectus of the Muslim Institute which illustrates one trend in the thinking of conservative Moslems:

> Muslims have for about 200 years suffered a period of continuous and rapid decline in all fields of human endeavor—economic, social, political, and intellectual—and have been surpassed by a rival and mostly hostile civilization of the West. . . .
>
> The Western civilization (including the communist experiment) has predictably failed to provide mankind with a viable framework for social harmony, moral and spiritual fulfillment and satisfaction, and international peace; Western civilization has in fact created more problems of greater complexity for mankind than those it may have solved. . . . The social relationship of Islam, on the other hand, would allow for even greater material well-being in a harmonious social order which is also free of conflicts between men, groups of men, factors of production, or

nations. . . . The Muslims' quest for "modernization" and "progress" through the Westernization of Muslim individuals and Muslim societies was, therefore, bound to fail and has done so at great cost to Muslim culture and the economic, social, and political fabric of Muslim societies. . . . The damage to Muslim societies is so extensive that it may not be possible or even desirable, to *repair* or *restore* their existing social orders; the only viable alternative is to *conceive* and *create* social, economic, and political systems which are fundamentally different from those now prevailing in Muslim societies throughout the world.[34]

Moslem intellectuals are actively seeking an "Islamic alternative" for their societies. In many countries young people belong to informal Islamic groups in which there is much discussion about the role and contribution of Islam to society. As one writer stated:

It is merely a historical accident that makes Islam appear to be struggling between two dominant ideologies [capitalism and Marxism]. For within the Islamic process itself there is a dynamic revitalizing force not only to keep Islam alive but which provides it with generative creativity to re-establish itself as a well-defined system with solutions that are original to current problems.[35]

Islamic law has exhibited an impressive elasticity and dynamism in recent years, since it allows for new interpretations and regulations as needed. King Fahd of Saudi Arabia has called for a revival of the principle of "ijtihad" ("fresh thinking") in Islamic law in order to examine in a modern light the meaning of some of Islam's most fundamental laws and tenets.[36]

It will be some time before all the effects of Islamic fundamentalism are felt; it is still a new social force. In a speech to a group of American businessmen in 1979, Dr. Algosaibi of Saudi Arabia described the movement in optimistic terms:

The revival of Islam is not to be feared or opposed. As Muslims find their true identitites, they will be much easier to understand, accept, and deal with.[37]

It is clear, however, that before that time comes, a great deal of confusion and upheaval will be experienced. The ambivalence toward or rejection of liberal social change can be better understood by considering the questions it raises in the mind of the modern Arab. How do you compare the relative value of a communications satellite with the wisdom of a village elder? What good is a son who is a computer expert but lacks filial respect? How do you cope with a highly-educated daughter who announces that she never intends to marry?

This is the context in which Westerners encounter Arabs today. Remembering it as you explore Arab culture and make contact and develop relationships with Arab acquaintances will help make your experience more comprehensible and the relationships you develop more rewarding.

1

Beliefs and Values

When we set ourselves the task of coming to a better understanding of groups of people and their culture, it is useful to begin by identifying their most basic beliefs and values. It is these beliefs and values which determine their outlook on life and govern their social behavior.

Westerners tend to believe, for instance, that the individual is the focal point of social existence, that laws apply equally to everyone, that people have a right to certain kinds of privacy, and that the environment can be controlled by humans through technological means. These beliefs have a strong influence on what Westerners think about the world around them and how they behave toward each other.

Arabs characteristically believe that many if not most things in life are controlled, ultimately, by fate rather than by humans, that everyone loves children, that wisdom increases with age, and that the inherent personalities of men and women are vastly different. As with Westerners, these beliefs play a powerful role in determining the nature of Arab culture.

One might wonder whether there is in fact such a thing as "Arab culture," given the diversity and geographic disparateness of the Arab World. Looking at a map, one realizes how much is encompassed by the phrase "the Arab World." The twenty Arab countries cover considerable territory, much of which is desert or wilderness. Sudan is larger than all of Western Europe, yet its population is less than that of France; Saudi Arabia is larger than Texas and Alaska combined, yet has fewer people than New York City. Egypt, with forty-two million people, is 95% desert. One writer has stated: "A true map of the Arab World would show it as an archipelago: a scattering of fertile islands through a void of sand and sea. The Arabic word for desert is 'sahara' and it both divides and joins."[1] The political diversity among the Arab countries is notable; governmental systems include monarchies, military governments, and socialist republics.

But despite these differences, the Arabs are more homogeneous than Westerners in their outlook on life. All Arabs share basic beliefs and values which cross national or social class boundaries. Social attitudes have remained relatively constant because Arab society is conservative and demands conformity from its members. Their beliefs are influenced by Islam even if they are not Moslems, child-rearing practices are nearly identical, and the family structure is essentially the same. Arabs are not as mobile as people in the West, and they have a high regard for tradition.

Initially foreigners may feel that Arabs are difficult to understand, that their behavior patterns are not logical. In fact their behavior is quite comprehensible, even predictable. For the most part it conforms to certain patterns which make Arabs consistent in their reactions to other people.

It is important for the foreigner to be able to identify these cultural patterns and to distinguish them from individual traits. By becoming aware of patterns, one can achieve a better understanding of what to expect and thereby cope more easily. The following lists of Arab values, religious attitudes and self-perceptions are central to the fundamental patterns of Arab culture and will be examined in detail in subsequent chapters.

Basic Arab Values

–A person's dignity, honor, and reputation are of paramount importance and no effort should be spared to protect them, especially one's honor.

–It is important to behave at all times in a way which will create a good impression on others.

–Loyalty to one's family takes precedence over personal needs.

–Social class and family background are the major determining factors of personal status, followed by individual character and achievement.

Basic Arab Religious Attitudes

–Everyone believes in God, acknowledges His power and has a religious affiliation.

–Humans cannot control all events; some things depend on God (i.e., "fate").

–Piety is one of the most admirable characteristics in a person.

–There should be no separation between "church and state"; religion should be taught in schools and promoted by governments.

–Religious tenets should not be subjected to "liberal" interpretations or modifications which can threaten established beliefs and practices.

Basic Arab Self-perceptions

–Arabs are generous, humanitarian, polite, and loyal. Several studies have demonstrated that Arabs see these traits as characteristic of themselves and as distinguishing them from other groups.[2]

–Arabs have a rich cultural heritage. This is illustrated by their contributions to religion, philosophy, literature, medicine, architecture, art, mathematics, and the natural sciences.[3]

–Although there are many differences among Arab countries, the Arabs are a clearly-defined cultural group, members of the "Arab nation" (al-umma al-'arabiyya).

–The Arab peoples have been victimized and exploited by the West. For them, the experience of the Palestinians represents the most painful and obvious example.

–Indiscriminate imitation of Western culture, by weakening traditional family ties and social and religious values, will have a corrupting influence on Arab society.

–Arabs are misunderstood and wrongly characterized by most Westerners.

Arabs feel that they are often portrayed in the Western media as excessively wealthy, irrational, sensuous, and violent, and there is little counterbalancing information about ordinary people who live family- and work-centered lives on a modest scale. One observer has remarked, "The Arabs remain one of the few ethnic groups who can still be slandered with impunity in America."[4] Another has stated, "In general, the image of the Arabs in British popular culture seems to be characterized by prejudice, hostility, and resentment. The mass media in Britain have failed to provide an adequate representation of points of view for the consumer to judge a real world of the Arabs."[5]

2

ٲ

Friends and Strangers

The Concept of Friendship

Relations between people are very personalized in the Arab culture. Friendships start and develop quickly. But the Arab concept of "friendship," with its rights and duties, is quite different from that in the West.

Westerners, especially North Americans, tend to think of a friend as someone whose company they enjoy. A friend can be asked for a favor or for help if necessary, but it is considered poor form to cultivate a friendship primarily for what can be gained from that person or his position. Among Arabs also, a friend is someone whose company they enjoy. However, *equally important to the relationship is the duty of a friend to give help and do favors to the best of his ability.*

Differences in expectations can lead to misunderstandings and, for both parties, a feeling of being let down. The Westerner thinks he has been "set up" to do favors, and the Arab concludes that no Westerner can be a "true friend." In order to avoid such feelings, we must bear in mind what is meant by both sides when one person tells the other that he is his "friend."

Reciprocal Favors

For an Arab, "good manners" require that one never openly refuse a request from a friend. This does not mean that the favor must actually be done, but rather that the response must not be stated as a direct "No." If a friend asks you for a favor, do it if you can—this keeps the friendship flourishing. If it is unreasonable, illegal, or too difficult, the correct form is to listen carefully and suggest that while you are doubtful about the outcome, you will at least try to help. Later, you express your regrets and offer to do something else for him in the future. In this way you have not openly refused a favor, and your face-to-face encounters have remained pleasant.

About five years ago I was talking to an Egyptian university student who told me that he was very disappointed in his American professor. The professor had gratefully accepted many favors while he was getting settled in Egypt, including assistance in finding a maid and buying furniture. When the Egyptian asked him to use his influence in helping him obtain a graduate fellowship in the U.S., the professor told him that there was no point in trying because his grades were not high enough to be competitive. The Egyptian took this as a personal affront and felt bitter that the professor did not care about him enough to help him work toward a better future. The more appropriate cross-cultural response by the professor would have been to make helpful gestures, for example, helping the student obtain information about fellowships, helping him with applications and offering encouragement, even if he was not optimistic about the outcome.

In 1974 an American military officer in Morocco became angry when his Moroccan neighbor asked him to buy some items from the local military exchange (PX), which is illegal. When he bluntly refused, his neighbor was offended and the friendship was severely damaged.

In Western culture actions are far more important and more valued than words. *In the Arab culture, an oral promise has its own value as a response.* If an action does not follow, the other person cannot be held entirely responsible for a "failure."

If you fail to carry out a request, you will notice that no matter how hopeful your Arab friend was that you would succeed, he will probably accept your regrets graciously without asking precisely why the favor could not be done (which could embarrass you and possibly force you to admit a failure). You should be willing to show the same forebearance and understanding in inquiring about one of your requests. Noncommital answers probably mean no hope. This is one of the most frustrating cultural patterns confronted by Westerners in the Arab World. You must learn to work with this idea rather than fighting against it.

When an Arab gives a "yes" answer to your request, he is not necessarily certain that the action will or can be carried out. Etiquette demands that your request have a positive *response.* The *result* is a separate matter. A positive response to a request is a declaration of intention and an expression of good will—no more than that. "Yes" should not always be taken literally. You will hear phrases such as "Inshallah" ("If God wills") used in connection with promised actions. This is called for culturally, and it sometimes results in lending a further degree of uncertainty to the situation.

In his controversial book, *The Arab Mind,* Dr. Raphael Patai discusses this characteristic in some detail:

> The adult Arab makes statements which express threats, demands, or intentions, which he does not intend to carry out but which, once uttered, relax emotional tension, give psychological relief and at the same time reduce the pressure to engage in any act aimed at realizing the verbalized goal. . . . Once the intention of doing something is verbalized, this *verbal* formulation itself leaves in the mind of the speaker the impression that he *has done* something about the issue at hand, which in turn psychologically reduces the importance of following it up by actually translating

the stated intention into action. . . . There is no "confusion" between words and action, but rather a psychologically conditioned substitution of words for action. . . . The verbal statement of a threat or an intention (especially when it is uttered repeatedly and exaggeratedly) achieves such importance that the question of whether or not it is subsequently carried out becomes of minor significance.[1]

Sometimes an Arab asks another person for something and then adds the phrase, "Do this for my sake." This phrasing sounds odd to a foreigner, especially if the persons involved do not know each other well, because it appears to imply a very close friendship. In fact, the expression means that the person requesting the action is acknowledging that he will consider himself indebted to return the favor in the future. "For my sake" is very effective in Arab culture when added to a request.

An Arab expects loyalty from anyone he considers a friend. The friend is therefore not justified in becoming indignant when asked for favors, since it should be understood from the beginning that giving and receiving favors is an inherent part of the relationship. Arabs will not form or perpetuate a friendship unless they also like and respect you; their friendship is not as calculated or self-serving as it may appear. The practice of cultivating a person only in order to "use" him is no more acceptable among Arabs than it is among Westerners.

Introductions

Arabs quickly determine another person's social status and connections when they meet. They will, in addition, normally give more information about themselves than Westerners do. They may indulge in a little (or a lot of) self-praise and praise of their relatives and family and present a detailed account of their social connections. When Westerners meet someone for the first time, they tend to confine personal information to generalities about their education, profession and interests.

To an Arab information about family and social connections is important, possibly even more important than the information about himself. Family information is also what he wants from you. He may find your response so inadequate that he wonders if you are hiding something, while your impression is that much of what he says is too detailed and largely irrelevant. Each person gives the information he thinks the other wants to know.

Your Arab friend's discourse about his "influence network" is *not* bragging, and it is *not* irrelevant. This information may turn out to be highly useful if you are ever in need of high-level personal contacts, and you should appreciate the offer of potential assistance from an "insider" in the community. Listen carefully to what he has to say.

Visiting Patterns

Arabs feel that good friends should see each other often, at least every few days, and they offer many invitations to each other. Westerners who have Arab friends sometimes feel overwhelmed and "crowded" by the frequent contact and wonder if they will ever have any privacy. There is no concept of "privacy" among Arabs. In translation, the Arabic word that comes closest to "privacy" means "loneliness"!

A British resident in Beirut once complained that he and his wife had almost no time to be alone—Arab friends and neighbors kept dropping in unexpectedly and often stayed late. He said, "I have one friend who telephoned and said, 'I haven't seen you anywhere. Where have you been for the last three days?'"

By far the most popular form of entertainment in the Arab

World is conversation. Arabs enjoy long discussions over shared meals or many cups of coffee or tea. You will be expected to reciprocate invitations, although you do not have to keep pace precisely with the number you receive. If you plead for "privacy" or become too slack in socializing, people will wonder if someone has offended you, if you don't like them, or if you are sick. You can say that you have become very busy, but resorting to this too often without sufficient explanation may be taken as an affront. "Perhaps," your friends may think, "he is just too busy for us."

I experienced a classic example of the Arab love of companionship in Cairo in 1978. After about three hours at a party where I was surrounded by loud music and louder voices, I stepped onto the balcony for a moment of quiet and fresh air. One of the women noticed and followed immediately, asking, "Is anything wrong? Are you angry at someone?"

If you are not willing to increase the frequency or intensity of your personal contacts, you may hurt your friends' feelings and damage the relationship. Ritual and essentially meaningless expressions used in Western greeting and leave taking, such as "We've got to get together sometime," may well be taken literally, and you have approximately a one-week grace period in which to follow up with an invitation before your sincerity is questioned.

Some Westerners, as they learn about the intricate and time-consuming relationships which develop among friends, decide that they would rather keep acquaintances at a distance. If you accept no favors, you will eventually be asked for none, and you will have much more time to yourself, but you will soon find that you have no Arab friends. An Arab friend is generous with his time and efforts to help you, is willing to inconvenience himself for you, and is concerned about your welfare. He will go to great lengths to be loyal and dependable. If you spend much time in an Arab country, it would be a great personal loss if you develop no Arab friendships.

Business Friendships

In business relationships personal contacts are much valued and quickly established. Arabs do not fit easily into impersonal roles, such as the "business colleague" role (with no private socializing offered or expected) or the "supervisor/employee" roles (where there may be cordial relations during work hours but where personal concerns are not discussed). All acquaintances are potential friends.

A good personal relationship is the most important single factor in doing business successfully with Arabs. A little light conversation before beginning a business discussion can be extremely effective in setting the right tone. Usually Arabs set aside a few minutes at the beginning of a meeting to inquire about each other's health and recent activities. If you are paying a business call on an Arab, it is best to let your host guide the conversation in this regard—if he is in a hurry, he may bring up the matter of business almost immediately; if not, you can tell by a lull in the conversational amenities when it is time to bring up the purpose of your visit. If an Arab is paying a call on you, don't be in such a rush to discuss business that you appear brusque.

The manager of the sales office of a British industrial equipment firm based in Kuwait told me about his initial inability to select effective salesmen. He learned that the best salesmen were not necessarily the most dapper, eager, or efficient. The most successful ones were those who were relaxed, personable, and patient enough to establish friendly personal relations with their clients.

You will find it useful to become widely acquainted in business circles and, if you learn to mix business with pleasure, you will soon see how the latter helps the former proceed. *In the end, personal contacts lead to more efficiency than following rules and regulations.* This is proven over and over again, when a quick telephone call to the right person cuts through lengthy procedures and seemingly insurmountable obstacles.

Office Relations

When Westerners work with the same people every day in an office, they sometimes become too casual about greetings. Arabs are conscientious about greeting everyone they see with "Good morning" or "Good afternoon" if it is the first meeting of the day, and they will go out of their way to say "Welcome back" when you return after an absence. Some Westerners omit greetings, especially if they are distracted or hurried, and Arab co-workers take notice. They usually understand and are not personally offended, but they take it as a lack of good manners.

In 1981 an American nurse at a hospital in Taif, Saudi Arabia, had an enlightening experience on an occasion when she telephoned her Saudi supervisor to report arrangements for an emergency drill. She was enumerating the steps being taken when the Saudi said, "That's fine, but just a moment—first of all, how are you today?"

If you bring food or snacks into the office, bring enough to share with everyone. Arabs place great value on hospitality and would be surprised if you ate or drank alone, without at least making an offer to share with everyone.

Remember to inquire about business colleagues and co-workers if they have been sick, and ask about their personal concerns from time to time. Arabs do mention the things which are happening in their lives, usually good things like impending trips, weddings, and graduations. You do not need to devote much time to this; it is the gesture that counts.

In Arab offices supervisors and managers are expected to give praise to their employees from time to time, to reassure them that their work is noticed and appreciated. Direct praise, such as, "You are an excellent employee and a real asset to this office," may be a little embarrassing to a Westerner, but Arabs give it frequently. You may hear, "I think you are a wonderful person, and I am so glad you are my friend," or "You are so intelligent and knowledgeable; I really admire you." Statements like this are meant sincerely and are very common.

I was once visiting an American engineering office in Riyadh and fell into conversation with a Jordanian translator. I asked him how he liked his work. He answered in Arabic so that the Americans would not understand, "I've been working here for four years. I like it fine, but I wish they would tell me when my work is good, not just when they find something wrong." Some Westerners assume that an employee knows he is appreciated simply because he is kept on the job, whereas Arab employees (and friends, for that matter) expect and want praise when they feel they have earned it. Even when the Westerner does offer praise, it may be insufficient in quantity or quality for the Arab subordinate.

Criticism

Arab employees usually feel that criticism of their work, if it is phrased too bluntly, is a personal insult. The foreign supervisor is well advised to take care in criticizing. He should be indirect and include praise of any good points first, accompanied by assurances of high regard for the individual himself. To preserve the person's dignity, avoid criticism in front of others, unless an "intermediary" is used (see below for further discussion of intermediaries). The concept of "constructive criticism" is truly not translatable into Arabic— forthright criticism is almost always taken as personal and destructive.

The need for care in criticism is well illustrated by an incident which occurred in an office in Amman in 1980. An American supervisor was discussing a draft report at some length with his Jordanian employee. He asked that more than half of it be rewritten, adding, "You must have entirely misunderstood what I wanted." The Jordanian was deeply hurt and said to one of the other employees, "I wonder why he doesn't like me." A far better approach would have been,

"You are doing excellent work here, and this is a good report. We need to revise a few things, however; let's look at this again and work through it together, so we can make it even better."

I remember overhearing a dramatic confrontation in an office in Tunis, when an American supervisor reprimanded a Tunisian employee because he continually arrived late. This was done in front of other employees, some of whom were his subordinates. The Tunisian flared up in anger and responded, "I am from a good family! I know myself and my position in society!" Clearly he felt that his honor had been threatened and was not even concerned with addressing the issue at hand.

In her perceptive book, *Temperament and Character of the Arabs,* Dr. Sania Hamady writes:

> Pride is one of the main elements on which Arab individualism rests, since it is sheer being which is primarily respected. To establish a good rapport with an Arab one must be aware of the fact that foremost in the Arab's view of the self is his self-esteem. It is important to pay tribute to it and to avoid offending it. The Arab is very touchy and his self-esteem is easily bruised. It is hard for him to be objective about himself or to accept calmly someone else's criticism of him . . . Facts should not be presented to him nakedly; they should be masked so as to avoid any molestation of his inner self, which should be protected.[2]

Intermediaries

The designation of one person to act as an intermediary between two other persons is very common in Arab society. Personal influence is very helpful in getting decisions made and things done, so people often ask someone with influence to represent them. (In Arabic an intermediary is called a "wasta.")

If you are a manager, you may find that some employees prefer to deal with you through another person, especially if that person knows you well. An intermediary may serve as a representative of someone with a request or as a negotiator between two parties in a dispute.

Mediation or representation through a third party also saves face in the event that a request is not granted, and it gives the petitioner confidence that maximum influence has been brought to bear. You may want to initiate this yourself if an unpleasant confrontation with someone appears necessary. But because you, as an outsider, could easily make a mistake in selecting an intermediary, it is best to consult with other Arab employees (of a higher rank than the person in question) in considering it. It would be wrong, for example, to choose an intermediary who has a lower social status than the person in question.

Foreign companies have local employees on their staff whose job is to maintain liaison with government offices and to help obtain permits and clearances. The better acquainted the employee is with government officials, the faster he can get the work done and the more likely he is to receive exceptional service when he asks. Arab "government relations" employees are indispensable; no foreigner could hope to be as effective with highly-placed officials.

You will observe the wide use of persons as intermediaries in Arab political disputes. Mediators, such as those who undertake "shuttle diplomacy," are often essential in establishing the personal contact that makes consensus possible. Their success depends on the quality of the personal relationship they establish with the parties involved. If a mediator is recognized by both parties as being honorable and trustworthy, he has already come a long way in solving the problem. That is why some negotiators and diplomats are far more effective than others; personalities and perceptions, not issues, determine their relative success.

An outstanding example of diplomatic success due, in large part, to personality may be seen in Henry Kissinger's achievements when he served as a negotiator between the leaders of Syria, Egypt, and Israel after the 1973 War. He established personal friendships with the individuals involved; Anwar Sadat's remark that "Dr. Henry is my friend" is very revealing. These friendships contributed greatly to Kissinger's ability to discuss complicated issues and keep a dialogue going, something no one had managed to do before.

Private and Public Manners

In the Arab way of thinking, people are clearly divided into friends and strangers. The manners required when dealing with each of these groups are very different. With friends and personal acquaintances, it is essential to be polite, honest, generous and helpful at all times. When dealing with strangers, "public manners" are applied and do not call for the same kind of considerateness.

It is accepted practice to do such things as crowd into lines, push, drive aggressively and overcharge tourists. If you are a stranger to the person or persons you are dealing with, then they will respond to you as they do to any stranger. Resenting this public behavior will not help you function better in Arab societies, and judging individuals as ill-mannered because of it will inhibit the development of needed relationships.

All over the Arab World people drive fast, cross lanes without looking, turn corners from the wrong lane, and honk their horns impatiently. Yet, if you catch a driver's eye or ask his permission, he will graciously motion for you to pull ahead of him or give you the right of way.

While shopping in a "tourist shop" in Damascus in 1978, I watched a busload of tourists buy items at extremely high prices. When they were gone, I chatted with the shopkeeper for a few minutes and bought some things. After I had left, a small boy came running after me—the shop owner had sent him to return a few more pennies in change.

Whenever I am in a crowded airport line, I try to make light conversation with the people around me. I have never had anyone with whom I visited try to push in front of me; in fact, they often motion for me to precede them.

Personal contact makes all the difference. If you feel jostled while you are waiting in line, the gentle announcement, "I was here first," or "Please wait in line," will usually produce an apology, and the person will at least stand behind *you*. Keep calm, avoid scenes, and remember that none of the behavior is directed at you personally.

3
٣

Emotion and Logic

How people deal with emotion or what value they place on objective vs. subjective behavior is culturally conditioned. *While objectivity is given considerable emphasis in Western culture, the opposite is true in Arab culture.*

Objectivity and Subjectivity

Westerners are taught that objectivity, the examination of facts in a logical way without the intrusion of emotional bias, is the mature and constructive approach to human affairs. One of the results of this belief is that in Western culture, subjectivity, a willingness to allow personal feelings and emotions to influence one's view of events, represents immaturity. Arabs believe differently. They place a higher value on the display of emotion, sometimes to the embarrassment or discomfort of foreigners. It is not uncommon to hear Westerners label this behavior as "immature," imposing their own values on what they have observed.

A British office manager in Saudi Arabia once described to me his problems with a Palestinian employee. "He is too sensitive, too emotional about everything," he said. "The first thing he should do is *grow up*." While Westerners label Arabs as "too emotional," Arabs find Westerners "cold" and inscrutable.

Arabs consciously reserve the right to look at the world in a subjective way, particularly if a more objective assessment of a situation would bring to mind a too-painful truth. There is nothing to gain, for example, by pointing out Israel's brilliant achievements in land reclamation or in comparing the quality of Arab-made consumer items with imported ones. Such comments will generally not lead to a substantive discussion of how Arabs could benefit by imitating others; more likely, Arab listeners will become angry and defensive, insisting that the situation is not as you describe it and bringing up issues such as Israeli occupation of Arab lands or the moral deterioration of technological societies.

Fatalism

Fatalism, or a belief that people are helpless to control events, is part of traditional Arab culture. It has been much over-emphasized by Westerners, however, and is far more prevalent among traditional, uneducated Arabs than it is among the educated elite today. It nevertheless still needs to be considered, since it will usually be encountered in one form or another by the Western visitor.

For Arabs, fatalism is based on the religious belief that God has direct and ultimate control of all that happens. If something goes wrong, a person can absolve himself of blame or justify doing nothing to make improvements or changes by assigning the cause to God's will. Indeed, too much self-confidence about controlling events is considered a sign of arrogance tinged with blasphemy. The legacy of fatalism in Arab thought is most apparent in the oft heard and more or less ritual phrase "Inshallah" (if God wills).

Western thought has essentially rejected fatalism. Though

God is believed by many Westerners to intervene in human affairs, Greek logic, the humanism of the Enlightenment and cause-and-effect empiricism have inclined the West to view humans as having the ability to control their environment and destinies.

What Is Reality?

Reality is what you perceive—if you believe something exists, it is real to you. If you select or rearrange facts, and repeat these to yourself often enough, they eventually become reality.

The cultural difference between Westerners and Arabs arises not from the fact that this selection takes place, but from how each makes the selection. *Arabs are more likely to allow subjective perceptions to direct their actions.* This is a common source of frustration for Westerners, who often fail to understand why people in the Middle East act as they do.

If an Arab feels that something threatens his personal dignity, he may be obliged to deny it, even in the face of facts to the contrary. A Westerner can point out flaws in his argument, but that is not the point. If he does not want to accept the facts, he will reject them and proceed according to his own view of the situation. An Arab will rarely admit to an error openly if it will cause him to lose face. *To Arabs, honor is more important than facts.*

An American woman in Tunis realized, when she was packing to leave, that some of her clothes and a suitcase were missing. She confronted the maid, who insisted that she had no idea where they could be. When the American found some of her clothes under a mattress, she called the company's Tunisian security officer. They went to the maid's house and found more missing items. The maid was adamant that she could not account for the items being in her home. The security officer said that he felt the matter should not be reported to the police—the maid's humiliation in front of her neighbors was sufficient punishment.

In 1974 an Israeli entered a small Arab-owned cafe in Jerusalem and asked for some watermelon, pointing at it and using the Hebrew word. The Arab proprietor responded that it should be called by the Arabic name, but the Israeli insisted on the Hebrew name. The Arab took offense at this point. He paused, shrugged, and instead of serving his customer, said, "There isn't any!"

At a conference held to discuss Arab and American cultures, Dr. Laura Nader related this incident:

> The mistake people in one culture often make in dealing with another culture is to transfer their functions to the other culture's functions. A political scientist, for example, went to the Middle East to do some research one summer and to analyze Egyptian newspapers. When he came back, he said to me, "But they are all just full of emotions. There is no data in these newspapers." I said, "What makes you think there should be?"[1]

Another way of influencing the perception of reality is by the choice of descriptive words and names. The Arabs are very careful in naming or referring to places, people, and events; slogans and labels are popular and provide an insight into how things are viewed. The Arabs realize that *names have a powerful effect on perception.*

There is a big psychological gap between opposing labels like "Palestine/Israel," "The West Bank/Judea and Samaria," and "freedom fighters ('hero martyrs' if they are killed)/terrorists." The 1967 Arab-Israeli War is called "The War of the Setback" in Arabic—in other words, it was *not* a "defeat." The 1973 War is called "The War of Ramadan" or "The Sixth of October War," *not* "The Yom Kippur War."

Be conscious of names and labels—they matter a great deal to the Arabs. If you attend carefully to what you hear in conversations with Arabs and what is written in their newspapers, you will note how precisely they select descriptive words and phrases. You may find yourself being corrected by Arab acquaintances, and you will soon learn which terms are acceptable and which are not.

The Human Dimension

ϒ Arabs look at life in a personalized way. They are concerned about people and feelings and place emphasis on "human factors" when they make decisions or analyze events. They feel that Westerners are too prone to look at events in an abstract or theoretical way, and that most Westerners lack sensitivity toward people.

In the Arab World, a manager or official is always willing to reconsider a decision, regulation, or problem in view of someone's personal situation. Any regulation can be modified or avoided by someone with enough persuasive influence, particularly if the request is justified on the grounds of unusual personal need. This is unlike most Western societies, which emphasize the equal application of laws to all citizens. *In the Arab culture, people are more important than rules.*

T.E. Lawrence stated it succinctly: "Arabs believe in persons, not in institutions."[2] They have a long tradition of personal appeal to authorities for exceptions to rules. This is commonly seen when they attempt to obtain special permits, exemptions from fees, acceptance into a school when preconditions are not met, or employment when qualifications are inadequate. They do not accept predetermined standards if these standards are a personal inconvenience.

Arabs place great value on personal interviews and on giving people the opportunity to state their case. They are not comfortable filling out forms or dealing with an organization impersonally. They want to know the name of the top person who makes the final decision and are always confident that the rejection of a request may be reversed if top-level personal contact can be made. Frequently, that is exactly what happens.

Persuasion

Arabs and Westerners place a different value on certain types of statements, which may lead to decreased effectiveness on both sides when they negotiate with each other. Arabs respond much more readily to personalized arguments than to attempts to impose "logical" conclusions. When you are trying to make a persuasive case in your discussions with Arabs, you will find it helpful to supplement your arguments with personal comments. You can refer to your mutual friendship, or emphasize the effect which approval or disapproval of the action will have on other people.

In the Middle East negotiation and persuasion have been developed into a fine art. Participants in negotiations enjoy long, spirited discussions and are usually not in any hurry to conclude them. Speakers feel free to add to their points of argument by demonstrating their verbal cleverness, using their personal charm, applying personal pressure, and engaging in personal appeals for consideration of their point of view.

The display of emotion also plays its part; indeed, one of the most commonly misunderstood aspects of Arab communication involves their "display" of anger. Arabs are not usually as angry as they appear to Westerners. Raising the voice, repeating points, even pounding the table for emphasis may sound angry but, in the speaker's mind, indicate sincerity. A Westerner overhearing such a conversation (especially if it is in Arabic) may wrongly conclude that an argument is taking place. *Emotion connotes deep and sincere concern for the outcome of the discussion.*

Foreigners often miss the emotional dimension in their cross-cultural transactions with Arabs. A British businessman once found that he and his wife were denied reservations on an airplane because the Arab ticketing official took offense at the manner in which he was addressed. The fact that seats were available was *not* an effective counter-argument. But when the Arab official noticed that the businessman's wife had begun to cry, he gave way and provided them with seats.

Arabs usually include human elements in their arguments. In arguing the Palestine issue, for instance, they have always placed emphasis on the suffering of individuals rather than on points of law or a recital of historical events.

4
ع

Getting Personal

The concept of what constitutes "personal" behavior or a "personal" question is culturally determined, and there are marked differences between Westerners and Arabs. This is a subject which is rarely discussed openly, since how one defines what is personal or private seems so natural to each group. On the whole, Westerners feel that Arabs become too personal, too soon.

Personal Questions

Arabs like to discuss money and may ask what you paid for things or what your salary is (this is more common among less Westernized people). If you don't wish to give out the information, consider "responding without answering." You can speak on the subject of money in general—how hard it is to stay ahead, high prices, inflation. After a few minutes of this, the listener will realize that you do not intend to give a substantive answer. This is the way an Arab would respond if he were asked a question he did not really want to answer.

If you are unmarried or if you are married and childless, or have no sons, Arabs may openly ask why. They consider it unusual for an adult to be unmarried, since marriage is arranged for most people by their families and is expected of everyone. They want children, especially sons, to enhance their prestige and assure them of care in their old age.

Unmarried people may well find themselves subjected to well-intentioned matchmaking efforts on the part of Arab friends. If you wish to avoid this, you may have to resort to making up a fictitious long-distance romance! You might say, "I hope to get married—I have someone in mind, and we're working out the plans. I hope it won't be long now." Statements such as "I'm not married because I haven't found the right person yet" or "I don't want to get married" make little sense to an Arab.

When you explain why you don't have children, or more children, unconvincing answers include "We don't want any more children" (impossible to believe), or "We can't afford more" (also doubtful). A more acceptable answer is "We would like more children and, if God wills, we will have more."

Questions which Arabs consider too personal are those pertaining to women in the family (if asked by a man). It is best to ask about "the family," not a person's wife, sister, or grown daughter.

Sensitive Subjects

There are two subjects which Arabs favor in social conversation—religion and politics—and both can be risky.

Moslems enjoy discussing religion with non-Moslem Westerners because of their curiosity about Western religious beliefs and because they feel motivated to share information about Islam with friends as a favor to them. They are secure in their belief about the "completeness" of Islam, since it is accepted as the third and final refinement of the two previously-revealed religions, Judaism and Christianity. They like to teach about Islam, which eventually leads to the question: Why don't you consider conversion? A Westerner may feel uncomfortable and wonder how to give a gracious refusal. The simplest, most gracious and acceptable answer is to state that you appreciate the information and respect Islam highly as a religion, but that you cannot consider conversion because it would offend your family.

Arabs like to talk politics with Westerners and readily bring up controversial issues like the Palestine problem and the legacy of colonialism and imperialism. Yet they are not prepared for frank statements of disagreement with their positions on these questions or even inadvertent comments which sound negative or supportive of the opposing side of the argument. The safest response, if you cannot agree fully, is to confine yourself to platitudes and wait for the subject to change, expressing your concern for the victims of war and your hope for a lasting peace. A frank, two-sided discussion is usually not constructive if the subject is an emotional one, and you may find that Arabs remember only the statements you made in support of "the other side."

You will be able to tell when you have brought up a sensitive subject by the way an Arab evades a direct answer to your questions. If you receive evasive answers, don't try to press further; there must be a reason why the person does not want to pursue the subject. John Laffin has described a discussion with the late Kamel Nasser, who was the press officer for the Palestine Liberation Organization:

> Nasser, a likeable but nervy man, put his hands to his head in despair. "Do you know, Arafat has never said either 'Yes' or 'No' to me when I ask him a direct question. You would think he could do that much for his Press officer!" I sympathized with him. "Do you like Arafat?" I asked. And Nasser replied, "It's not a matter of liking or disliking. . . ."
>
> In my three long talks with him [Nasser] he, too, never once said "Yes or "No."[1]

Social Distance

Arab and Western cultures differ in the amount of touching they practice in interpersonal relations and in the physical distance they maintain when conversing. These norms are largely unconscious, so both Arabs and Westerners may feel uncomfortable without knowing exactly why.

In general, Arabs tend to stand and sit closer and to touch other people (of the same sex) more than Westerners do. It is common to see two men or two women holding hands as they walk down a street, which is simply a sign of friendship. A Westerner must be prepared for the possibility that an Arab will take his hand, especially when crossing the street. After shaking hands in greeting an Arab may continue to hold the other person's hand while talking if the conversation is expected to be brief. He will then shake it again when saying goodbye. Kissing on both cheeks is a common form of greeting (again, only with members of the same sex), as is embracing. It is also common to touch someone repeatedly during a conversation, often to emphasize a point. Children, especially if they are blond, should be prepared to have their heads rubbed by well-meaning adults.

Arab culture does not have the same concept of "public" and "private" space as Western cultures. Westerners, in a sense, carry a little bubble of private space around with them. Arabs, on the other hand, are not uncomfortable when they are close to or touching strangers.

Westerners are accustomed to standing in an elevator in such a way that maximum space is maintained between people. In the Arab world it is common for a person to board an elevator and stand close beside you rather than moving to the opposite corner. When an Arab boards a bus or selects a seat on a bench, he often sits beside someone rather than going to an empty seat or leaving a space between himself and others. This tendency was particularly annoying to an American who was standing on a street corner in Beirut waiting for a friend. He had a good view of the intersecting streets until a Lebanese man came to the corner and, apparently also waiting for someone, stood directly in front of him. The American could see no rationale for the Lebanese standing so close.

When Arabs and Westerners are talking, they may both continually shift position, each trying to maintain a comfortable distance as the Arab approaches and the Westerner backs away. For Arabs the space which is comfortable for ordinary social conversation is approximately the same as that which Westerners reserve for intimate conversation.

Anthropologist Edward Hall has described the Arab concept of personal space as follows:

> For the Arab, there is no such thing as an intrusion in public. Public means public. In the Western world, the person is synonymous with an individual inside a skin. And in northern Europe generally, the skin and even the clothes may be inviolate. You need permission to touch either if you are a stranger. . . . For the Arab, the location of the person in relation to the body is quite different. The person exists somewhere down inside the body. . . . Tucking the ego down inside the body shell not only would permit higher population densities but would explain why it is that Arab communications are stepped up as much as they are when compared to northern European communication patterns. Not only is the sheer noise level much higher, but the piercing look of the eyes, the touch of the hands, and the mutual bathing in the warm moist breath during conversation represent stepped-up sensory inputs to a level which many Europeans find unbearably intense.[2]

Robert Barakat, in a study of Arab gestures, also discusses Arab "body language":

> All Arabs . . . share a certain basic vocabulary of body language. They stand close together and frequently touch each other in a conversation, and they look each other in the eye constantly, instead of letting their gaze drift to the side as Americans do.[3]

You do not need to adopt Arab touching patterns, of course; just be aware that they are different from your own and accept them as natural and normal for Arabs. Note: in Saudi Arabia and the Arabian Peninsula countries, touching other people is done much less and can even be offensive.

Gestures

Arabs make liberal use of gestures when they talk, especially if they are enthusiastic about what they are saying. Hand and facial gestures are thus an important part of Arab communication, and you should be able to recognize them in order to get the full meaning of what is being said to you.

Listed here are some of the most common gestures used in Arab countries. There are variations among countries, but most are in wide use. Men use gestures more than women, and less-educated people use them more than the educated. It is not recommended that you *use* these gestures (foreigners often use gestures in the wrong place or situation) but that you learn to *recognize* them.

1. Move the head slightly back and raise the eyebrows: No. Move the head back and chin upward: No. Move the chin back slightly and make a clicking sound with the tongue: No.

2. After shaking hands, place the right hand to the heart or chest: Greeting with respect or sincerity.

3. Hold the right hand out, palm downward, and move it as if scooping something away from you: Go away.

4. Hold the right hand out, palm upward, and open and close the hand: Come here.

5. Hold the right hand out, palm upward, then close the hand halfway and hold it: Give it to me.

6. Hold the right hand out, palm downward, and move it up and down slowly: Quiet down.

7. Hold the right hand out, palm upward, and touch the thumb and tips of fingers together, then move the hand up and down: Calm down; Be patient; Slowly.

8. Hold the right forefinger up and move it from left to right quickly several times: No; Never.

9. Hold the right hand out, palm downward, then quickly twist the hand to show the palm upward: What? Why?

10. Make a fist with the right hand, keeping the thumb extended upward: Very good; I am winning. (This is a victory sign. You may have seen this gesture made by Yasser Arafat when talking to the press.)

Names

In many Western societies, one indication of the closeness of a personal relationship is the use of first names. In Arab society, the first name is used immediately, even if it is preceded by "Miss," "Mrs." or "Mr."

Arabs do not refer to people by their third, or "last," name. Arab names, for both men and women, are comprised of a first name (the person's own), their father's name, and their paternal grandfather's name, followed by a family name (in countries where family names are used). In other words an Arab's name is simply a string of names listing ancestors on the father's side. It would be the same as if a Westerner's name were John (given name) Robert (his father) William (his grandfather) Jones.

Because names reflect genealogy on the father's side, women have masculine names after their first name. Some people include "ibn" (son of) or "bint" (daughter of) between the ancestral names. This practice is common in the Arabian Peninsula; for example, Abdel-Aziz ibn Saud (son of Saud), the founder of the Kingdom of Saudi Arabia. In North Africa the word "ben" or "ould" is used to mean "son of," and "bou" which means "father of" is also a common element of a family name. Examples are Chadli Bendjedid, the President of Algeria, Mohamed Khouna Ould Haidalla, President of Mauritania, and Habib Bourguiba, former President of Tunisia.

Because a person's first name is the only one which is really his or hers, Arabs use it from the moment they are introduced. A Western man can expect to be called "Mr. Bill" or "Mr. John." If he is married, his wife will be called "Mrs. Mary," or possibly "Mrs. Bill." First names are also used with titles, such as "Doctor" and "Professor."

A person may retain several names for legal purposes, but often omit them in daily use. A man named Ahmad Abdallah Ali Mohamed would be commonly known as Ahmad Abdallah; if he has a family or tribal name such as Al-Harithi, he would be known as Ahmad Abdallah Al-Harithi, or possibly Ahmad Al-Harithi. People are not always consistent when reciting their names on different occasions.

When a genealogical name becomes too long (after four or five generations), some of the names will be dropped, generally in reverse order. The only pattern which is really consistent is that the father's name will be retained, and the family name if there is one. It is entirely possible that full brothers and sisters may be registered with different combinations of names.

In Arabian Peninsular countries telephone books list people under their family names. In some Arab countries, however, the telephone book lists people under their first names, because the first name is the only one which can be depended upon to be consistently present. Some business organizations find it easier to keep payroll records by first name.

A family or tribal name identifies a large extended family or group whose members still consider themselves tied by bonds of kinship and honor. A family name may be geographical (Hijazi, "from Hijaz"; Halaby, "from Aleppo"); denote an occupation (Haddad, "smith"; Najjar, "carpenter"); be descriptive (Al-Ahmar, "red"; Al-Tawil, "tall"); denote tribe (Al-Harithi; Quraishi); or sound like a personal name because it is the name of a common ancestor (Abdel-Aziz; Ibrahim).

An Arab woman does not change her name after marriage, since she cannot take her husband's genealogy, which is what it would imply. Besides, Arabs are very proud of their mother's family and want her to retain the name and refer to it. Only informally is a wife called "Mrs." with her husband's first or last name.

When people have children, an informal but very pleasing and polite way to address them is "father of" (abu) or "mother of" (umm) the oldest son or oldest child, as in Umm Ahmad, "mother of Ahmad." It is considered respectful, and is especially useful when talking to a woman, as it provides a less personal way of addressing her.

Arabs do not name their sons after the father, but naming a child after his paternal grandfather is common. You will meet many men whose first and third names are the same.

Titles are used more widely in Arabic than in English. Anyone with an M.D. or Ph.D. degree must be addressed as "Dr." ("duktoar" for a man, "duktoara" for a woman). It is important to find out any titles a person may have; omitting the title can be insulting. "Sheikh" is a respectful title for a wealthy, influential or elderly man. Government ministers are called "Excellency" (Ma'ali) and senior officials are given the honorary title "Sa'ada" before their other titles and name.

A person's name can be a clue to certain facts about him. Many names indicate religion or country of origin. This explains why some people introduce themselves with various long combinations of names, especially if their first and last names are ambiguous (used by more than one group).

It is useful for foreigners to be able to "place" people, at least partially, upon hearing their names. Here are a few guidelines.

1. If a name sounds Western (George, William, Mary), it marks a Christian.

2. If a name is that of a well-known figure in Islamic history (Mohamed, Bilal, Salah-Eddeen, Fatma, Ayesha), it marks a Moslem.

3. Most hyphenated names using "Abdel-" are Moslem. The name means "Servant (Slave) of God," and the second part is one of the attributes of God (Abdallah, "Servant of Allah"; Abdel-Rahman, "Servant of the Merciful"; Abdel-Karim, "Servant of the Generous"). There are a few Christian names on this pattern (Abdel-Malak, "Servant of the Angel"; Abdel-Massih, "Servant of the Messiah"), but over 90% of the time you can assume that a person with this type of name is Moslem. Moslems list 99 attributes for God altogether (All-Powerful, All-Knowing, Compassionate, All-Wise, etc.), and most of these are presently in use as names.

4. Names containing the word "Deen" (religion) are Moslem (Sharaf-Eddeen, "The Honor of Religion"; Badr-Eddeen, "The Moon of Religion"; Sayf-Eddeen, "The Sword of Religion").

5. Most Arab names have a meaning, so many are simply descriptive adjectives (Aziz, "dear"; Said, "happy"; Amin, "faithful"; Hasan, "good"). Such descriptive names do not mark religion.

6. Names which are both Koranic and Biblical (Ibrahim, "Abraham"; Sulaiman, "Solomon"; Daoud, "David"; Yousef, "Joseph") do not mark religion.

5

Men and Women

In Arab society the nature of interaction between men and women depends on the situation. Continual interaction is expected at work or in professional situations (although it remains reserved by Western standards, and in Saudi Arabia is actually restricted), but social interaction is very carefully controlled. The degree of control differs among Arab countries, depending on their relative conservatism, but nowhere is it as free and casual as in Western societies, and in Saudi Arabia it is quite stringent.

Social Interaction

The maintenance of family honor is one of the highest values in Arab society. Since misbehavior by women can do more damage to family honor than misbehavior by men, clearly defined patterns of behavior have been developed to protect women and help them avoid situations which may give rise to false impressions or unfounded gossip. Women interact freely only with other women and close male relatives.

Arab men and women are careful about appearances when they meet. They must never permit themselves to be alone together, not even for a short time. They would find it improper to be in a room together with the door closed, to go out on a date as a couple, or to travel together, even on a short daytime trip. Shared activities take place with other people present. At mixed social events women are accompanied by their husbands or male relatives. It is customary in Saudi Arabia for "religious police" to question couples who are at a restaurant or in a car together and ask for proof that they are married.

Foreigners must be aware of the restrictions which pertain to contacts between men and women and then consider their own appearance in front of others. *Arabs quickly gain a negative impression if you behave with too much (presumed) familiarity toward a person of the opposite sex.* They will interpret your behavior on their own terms and may conclude that you are a person of low moral standards. If an embarrassing incident involves a Western man and an Arab woman, they may feel that the Westerner insulted the woman's honor, thereby threatening the honor of her family.

A Western man can feel free to greet an Arab woman at a social gathering (again, this is not the common practice in Saudi Arabia), but it is best if their subsequent discussion includes other people rather than just the two of them. A Western woman can feel free to greet and visit with Arab men, provided that she is accompanied by her husband. If a woman is unmarried or if her husband is not present, she should be more reserved. In many Arab countries men and women separate into their own conversation groups shortly after arrival at a social gathering; this depends on the customs of a given area. In Saudi Arabia women are often excluded from social gatherings altogether or may be more restricted in their behavior when they are not. Social separation is not practiced merely because it is required by custom; it is often preferred by both men and women because they feel more comfortable. Westerners can expect to spend much of their social time in all-male or all-female groups.

Western men and women should give thought to their appearance in front of others when they interact among themselves. Behavior such as overly enthusiastic greetings, animated and joking conversations, and casual invitations to lunch are easily misinterpreted by Arabs and reinforce their stereotype of the morally lax Westerner.

Displaying Intimacy

The public display of intimacy between men and women is strictly forbidden by the Arab social code, including holding hands or linking arms or any gesture of affection such as kissing or prolonged touching. Such actions, even between husband and wife, are highly embarrassing to Arab observers. In 1975 a married couple were asked to leave a theater in Cairo because they were seen holding hands.

This type of behavior is a particularly serious offense in Saudi Arabia. In 1983 an American woman was observed getting into a car with an American man, sliding over to his side, and kissing him on the cheek. The captain of the Saudi National Guard who saw this demanded proof that they were married. They were, but not to each other. The woman was sent out of the country and the man, who compounded his problem by being argumentative, was sent to jail.

Even if you see behavior such as hand-holding (especially among young people in the less traditional countries), it is useful to know that it is still viewed by most people with disapproval.

The Status of Women

The degree to which women have been integrated into the work force and circulate freely in public varies widely among the Arab countries. In Lebanon, Jordan, and Egypt, educated women are very active at all levels of society. In Saudi Arabia, Yemen, and the Arabian Gulf states, few women have jobs outside the home; those who do, work only in all-female environments such as schools and banks for women, with the exception of those in the medical professions.

All Arab governments now strongly support efforts to increase women's educational opportunities. In 1956, many years before the issue gained its current prominence, the Tunisian President, Habib Bourguiba, instituted laws improving the legal status of women and ultimately became known as "Liberator of Women." Iraq revised personal status laws regarding marriage, child custody, and inheritance in 1959. Egypt has drastically revised laws concerning marriage and divorce; for example, an Egyptian woman can now sue for divorce if her husband takes a second wife without her permission, and in Morocco a woman can stipulate in her marriage contract that polygamy is grounds for divorce.[1] In the past ten to twenty years, personal status laws have been revised to increase the legal rights of women in most Arab countries, either by supplementing or reinterpreting traditional Islamic law. In virtually every Arab country today, the laws regarding women are being discussed and are imminently subject to change.

Do not assume that because the role of Arab women is not highly visible in public their influence is similarly diminished in private life. In traditional Arab society men and women have well-defined spheres of activity and influence. Men are responsible for providing for the family's material welfare. Even if a woman has money, she need not contribute to family expenses. Most women in fact *do* have their own money, and Islamic religious law states clearly that they retain sole control over their money and inheritance after marriage.

Arab women have a good deal of power in decision-making. They usually have the decisive voice in matters relating to household expenditures, the upbringing and education of children, and sometimes the arrangement of marriages.

The older a woman becomes, the more status and power she accrues. Men owe great respect to their mothers all their lives, and most men make every effort to obey their mother's wishes, even her whims. All older women in a family are treated with deference. A woman who is the mother of sons gains even more status.

Moslem women veil their faces, wholly or partially, in conservative countries such as Saudi Arabia, Kuwait, the Arabian Gulf states, Yemen, and Libya, and to some degree in Morocco, Algeria, and Tunisia (this varies, depending on a woman's age and social class.) Veiling has almost disappeared, except in rural areas or in very conservative families in such countries as Syria, Lebanon, Jordan, and Iraq. The Koran itself says nothing about veiling although it does urge women to be modest in their dress. Veiling has always been a matter of local custom, not a religious requirement. You will notice that Arab women wear clothing which is at least knee-length and partially sleeved and often cover their hair. The practice of wearing floor-length, fully-sleeved clothing is increasing, not decreasing, even in modern cities like Cairo and Amman, because of the increased influence of Islamic fundamentalism.

Tradition-oriented Arab men and women do not view the social customs and restrictions as repressive, but as complimentary to the status and nature of women. They see the restrictions as providing *protection* for women so that they need not be subjected to the stress, competition, temptations, and possible indignities present in "outside" society. Most Arab women feel satisfied that the present social system provides them with security, protection, and respect.

Some women, however, view their situation otherwise, and have begun pressing for greater social, legal, and personal freedom. There is a clear trend toward relaxing some of the restrictions which have regulated women's activities. It is important for an outsider to keep both points of view in mind when analyzing or discussing this subject.

Western Women

Western women find that they do not quite fit into Arab society; they are not accorded the rights of men but they are not considered bound by all the restrictions of Arab women either.

Western women are expected to behave with propriety, but they are not required to be as conservative as Arab women in dress or in public behavior. They need not veil in Saudi Arabia, for example, but must wear conservative street dress in all Arab countries. They may go shopping, attend public activities or travel alone. On the other hand, in Saudi Arabia they cannot drive.

Arabs accept professional Western women and admire them for their accomplishments. Well-educated women find that their opinions are taken seriously, and they are often invited to all-male professional gatherings. When a woman has a work-related reason to call on someone or to be present at any event, she is almost always welcomed, and men are comfortable with her.

6

Social Formalities and Etiquette

Social formalities and rules of etiquette are extremely important in Arab society. *Good manners constitute the most salient factor in evaluating a person's character.*

Hospitality

Arabs are generous in the hospitality they offer to friends and strangers alike and admire and value the same in others. *Generosity to guests is essential for a good reputation.* It is an insult to characterize someone as "stingy" or "inhospitable."

Arabs assume the role of host or hostess whenever the situation calls for it—in their office, home, or shop. A guest never stays long without being offered something to drink, and it is assumed that the guest will accept at least a small quantity as an expression of friendship or esteem. No matter how much coffee or tea the guest has had elsewhere, this offer is never declined. Shops and business offices have employees whose sole duty is to serve beverages to guests. When you are served a beverage, accept and hold the cup or glass with your right hand.

Dr. Fathi Yousef, an Arab sociologist, has pointed out that a North American would likely ask guests, "Would you care for coffee or tea?" using an intonation pattern which suggests that they may or may not want any refreshment. A Middle Easterner would ask, "What would you like—coffee or tea?" simply giving the guests a choice.[1] If someone comes to a home or place of business while food is being served, the people eating always offer to share the food. Usually an unexpected guest declines, but the gesture must be made.

The phrase "Welcome" ("Ahlan wa Sahlan" or "Marhaba") is used when a guest arrives, and it is repeated several times during a visit. A guest is often given a seat of honor (this is particularly common as a gesture to a foreigner), and solicitous inquiries are made about his comfort during the visit. A typical description of Arab hospitality appears in the introduction to a phrasebook entitled *Spoken Arabic:*

> Hospitality is a byword among [Arabs], whatever their station in life. As a guest in their homes you will be treated to the kindest and most lavish consideration. When they say, as they often do, "My home is your home," they mean it.[2]

Regardless of pressing circumstances, an Arab would never consider refusing entrance to a guest, even if he is unexpected and the visit is inconvenient. The only excusable circumstance would be if a woman (or women) were at home alone when a man dropped by—and then it would be the *visitor* who would refuse to enter, even if his prospective host were expected back very soon.

Arabs are proud of their tradition of hospitality and have many anecdotes illustrating it. A favorite is the story of the Bedouin who killed his last camel to feed his guest. Arabs expect to be received with hospitality when they are guests, and *your personal image and status will be affected by people's perceptions of your hospitality.*

The most important components of hospitality are welcoming a guest (including using the word "Welcome"), offering a seat (in many Arab homes, there is a special room set aside for receiving guests, called the "salon"), and offering something to drink. As a host, stay with your guests as much as possible, excusing yourself for brief absences from the room as necessary.

Fathi Yousef provides a close-up view of how Arabs receive guests:

> Although the "salon" is a very important room in the home, it is not the most frequently used. It is, paradoxically, both focal and peripheral. It is the center of the family's formal social interactions with visitors, while it is physically located on the periphery of the home. . . . In such a layout, the guest knocks at the door and is led into the "salon" through the home or asked to please wait until the other door leading immediately to the "salon" is opened for him. The behavior reflects two of the primary cultural values of the area. The first is the preoccupation with the concept of face, facades, and appearances. The guest is exposed only to the most shining, formal, and stylized part of the home and gets to meet only the members whom the family intends for him to meet. On the other hand, relationships in the Middle East reflect contextual varieties of guest-host interactions with territorial expectations of welcome and hospitality on the part of the guest and situational obligations of maintaining the traditional image of an open house on the part of the host. Thus, in receiving the guest in the most distinguished part of the home and in having him meet only the members of the family dressed for the occasion, the guest is honored and the family status is reflected.[3]

Even as a tourist, you will be met with hospitality in the Arab World. If you ask directions, people will try to give you an answer (even if they don't know what it is!), or they will assist you in asking others, or they may even take you to your destination themselves.

A friend of mine once made up a fictitious address in Riyadh and asked several people where it was; he got an answer every time. The crowning moment came when he asked two policemen, who simultaneously pointed in opposite directions.

In Tunis, Cairo, Beirut, and Amman I have asked for

directions and been escorted to my destination even though it was a long walk and a considerable inconvenience for my guide. When thanking someone for such a favor, you will hear the response, "No thanks are needed for a duty." No task is too burdensome for a hospitable host.

Time and the Keeping of Appointments

Among Arabs, time is not as fixed and rigidly segmented as it tends to be among Westerners. It flows from past to present to future, and Arabs flow with it. Social occasions and even appointments need not have fixed beginnings or endings. Arabs are thus much more relaxed about the timing of events than they are about other aspects of their lives. Nevertheless, these attitudes are beginning to change as Arabs respond to the demands of economic and technological development and modernization.

Some Arabs are careful to arrive on time (and are impatient with those who do not), and some are habitually late, especially for social events. Given these attitudes, a person who arrives late and has kept you waiting may not even realize that you have been inconvenienced and expect an apology.

Frequently, an Arab shopkeeper or someone in a service trade fails to have something done by a promised time. Be flexible; everyone expects delays. You will appear unreasonably impatient and demanding if you insist on having things finished at a precise time. This pertains to public services (such as getting a telephone connected), personal services, bus and train departures, customer services (where standing in long lines can be expected) and bureaucratic procedures.

If you invite people for dinner or a social event, do not expect all of your guests to arrive on time. A dinner should be served rather late and social plans should always be flexible enough to accommodate late-arriving guests.

The Arabic word "Ma'alish" represents an entire way of looking at life and its frustrations. It means "Never mind," or

"It doesn't matter," or even "Excuse me—it's not that serious." You will hear this said frequently when someone has had a delay, a disappointment, or an unfortunate experience. Rather than give in to pointless anger, Arabs often react to impersonally caused adversity with resignation and, to some extent, an acceptance of their fate.

Discussing Business

Arabs mistrust people who do not appear to be sincere or who fail to demonstrate an interest in them personally or in their country. They also don't like to be hurried or to feel they are being pressured into a business agreement. If they like you, they will agree to try to work out an arrangement or a compromise; if they do not like you, they will probably stop listening. They evaluate the *source* of a statement or proposal as much as the *content*.

Initial reactions by your Arab counterparts to your suggestions, ideas, and proposals can be quite misleading if taken at face value. An Arab is not likely to criticize openly. He is more likely to hint that changes are needed or give more subtle indications that the proposal is unacceptable—by inaction, for instance. He may promise to be in touch but fail to do so. Or he may offer a radical counterproposal, which may constitute a position from which compromise is expected. Watch out for flattery and praise, which will more likely be adherence to good manners than an indicator of potential success in the business transaction. Some decisions simply require consultation with superiors if you are not dealing with the top person. A noncommittal reaction to a proposal does not mean its rejection, nor does it guarantee ultimate acceptance. Only time will tell the outcome, with success dependent, more often than not, on patience and the cultivation of good personal relations.

Despite the frustration you may feel as the result of delays, *if you press for a specific time by which you want a decision, you may actually harm your chances of success.* Your counterpart may perceive it as an insult, especially if he is high-ranking.

The vice president of an American engineering company was meeting with a high-level Saudi official in the Ministry of Planning in Riyadh. The American's local representative had been trying for several weeks to obtain from the Ministry approval of one of the company's proposals. The vice president decided at the meeting to request that the Ministry give them a definite answer during the week he was to be in town. The Saudi looked surprised and appeared irritated, and answered that he could not guarantee action in that time. The proposal was never approved.

If a decision is coming slowly, it may mean that the proposal needs to be reassessed. Do not expect to conclude all of your business at once, especially if several decisions are required. Patience and repeated visits are called for. Arabs have plenty of time, and they see little need to accommodate foreigners who are in a hurry.

Sharing Meals

Arabs enjoy inviting guests to their home for meals; you will probably be a guest at meals many times. Meals provide an Arab host and hostess with a perfect opportunity to display their generosity and demonstrate their personal regard for you.

It is not an Arab custom to send written invitations or to request an "RSVP" confirmation of acceptance. Invitations are usually verbal and often spontaneous.

If it is your first invitation, check with others for the time meals are usually served and for the time you are expected to arrive. Westerners often arrive too early and expect the meal to be served earlier than is customary. In most Arab countries, a large midday meal is served between 2:00 and 3:00 p.m., and a supper (with guests) is served about 10:00 or 11:00 p.m. Guests should arrive about two hours before the meal—most of the conversation takes place before the meal, not after it. If the dinner is formal and official, you may be expected to arrive at the specified time and you can expect the meal to end within an hour or two.

Arabs serve a great quantity of food when they entertain—indeed, they are famous for their munificence and very proud of it. They usually prepare two or three times more food than the guests can eat. They do not try to calculate the amount of food actually needed; on the contrary, the intention is to present abundant food, which displays generosity and esteem for the guests. (The food does not go to waste; it is consumed by the family or by servants for several days afterwards.)

Most foreigners who have experienced an Arab meal have their favorite "hospitality" stories. In 1980 a banquet was given by a wealthy merchant in Qatar, who was known for his largesse. After several courses the guests were served an entire sheep—one per person!

You can expect to be offered second and third helpings of food, and you should make the gesture at least once of accepting. Encouraging guests to eat is part of an Arab host or hostess's duty and is required for good manners. This encouragement to eat more is called "'uzooma" in Arabic, and the more traditional the Arab, the more insistently it is done. Guests often begin with a ritual refusal and allow themselves to be won over by the host's insistence. You will hear:

"No, thanks."
"Oh, but you must!"
"No, I really couldn't!"
"You don't like the food!"
"Oh, but I do!"
"Well then, have some more!"

Water may not be served until after a meal is finished; some people consider it unhealthy to eat and drink at the same time. In any case Arab food is rarely "hot," although it may be highly seasoned.

A guest is expected to express admiration and gratitude for the food. Because you are trying to be polite, you will probably overeat. Many people eat sparingly on the day they are invited out to dinner because they know how much food will be served that evening.

In Morocco a table is often set with several tablecloths, and one is removed after every course. Before you begin to eat, count the tablecloths!

When you have eaten enough, you may refuse more by saying "Alhamdu lillah" (Thanks be to God). When the meal is over and you are about to leave the table, it is customary to say "Dayman" (Always) or "Sufra dayma" (May your table always be thus) to the host and hostess. The most common responses are "Ti'eesh" (May you live) and "Bil hana wa shifa" (To your happiness and health).

After a meal Arabs serve tea or coffee, often pre-sweetened. Conversation continues for a while longer, perhaps an hour, and then guests prepare to leave. In some countries bringing a tray of ice water around is a sign that dinner is over and the guests are free to leave. In the Arabian Peninsula countries incense or cologne may be passed around just before the guests depart.

When guests announce their intention to leave, the host and hostess usually exclaim, "Stay a while—it's still early!" This offer is ritual; you may stay a few more minutes, but the expression need not be taken literally and it does not mean that you will give offense by leaving. Generally you can follow the example of other guests, except that many Arabs prefer to stay out very late, so you may still be the first to leave! In most Arab countries you do not have to stay after midnight.

When you are invited to a meal, it is appropriate, although not required, to bring a small gift. The most common gifts are flowers and candy.

If you invite Arabs to your home, consider adopting some of their mealtime customs; it will improve their impression of you.

In the countries of the Arabian Peninsula, women rarely go out socially. When you invite a man and his wife to your home, the wife may not appear. It depends largely on whether the couple is accustomed to socializing with foreigners and on who else will be there. It is considerate, when a man is inviting a couple, to say, "My wife invites your wife" and to volunteer information about who else is invited. This helps the husband decide whether he wishes his wife to meet the other guests, and it assures him that other women will be present. Don't be surprised if some guests do not come, or if someone arrives with a friend or two.

Always serve plenty of food, with two or three main meat dishes; otherwise you may give the impression of being stingy.

I once heard an Egyptian describe a dinner at an American's home where the guests were served one large steak apiece. "They counted the steaks, and they even counted the potatoes," he said. "We were served baked potatoes—one per person!"

If you serve buffet style rather than a seated dinner with courses, your eating schedule will be more flexible and the visual impression of the amount of food served will be enhanced.

Give thought to your menu, considering which foods are eaten locally and which are not. Serve foods in fairly simple, easily-recognizable form so guests won't wonder what they are eating in a foreigner's home. Arabs usually do not care for sweetened meats, or for sweet salads with the main meal.

Moslems are forbidden to eat pork. Some foreigners serve pork (as one of the choices at a buffet) and label it; this is not advisable since it can be disconcerting to Moslems, who may wonder if the pork has touched any of the rest of the food.

The consumption of alcohol is also forbidden for Moslems. Do not use it in your cooking unless you label or mention it. Cooking with wine or other alcohol will limit the dishes available to your Moslem guests—it does not matter that the alcohol may have evaporated during cooking. If you wish to serve wine or alcoholic beverages, have non-alcoholic drinks available too.

Be sure to offer your guests second and third helpings of food. You don't have to insist vigorously, but you should make the gesture. Serve coffee and tea at the end of a meal.

When guests leave, accompany them all the way to the outer door of an apartment building or to the outer gate of your house.

Smoking

The overwhelming majority of Arab adults smoke, although women seldom smoke in public. Smoking is considered an integral part of adult behavior and it constitutes, to some extent, the expression of an individual's "coming of age." Arab men, in particular, view smoking as a right, not a privilege. Do not be surprised if you see people disregarding "No Smoking" signs in airplanes, waiting rooms, or elevators.

Arabs are rarely aware that smoking may be offensive to some Westerners. You can ask someone to refrain from smoking by explaining that it bothers you, but he may light up again after a few minutes. If you press the point too strongly, you will appear unreasonable.

Rules of Etiquette

Listed here are some of the basic rules of etiquette in Arab culture.

It is important to sit properly. Slouching, draping the legs over the arm of a chair, or otherwise sitting carelessly when talking with someone communicates a lack of respect for that person. Legs are never crossed on top of a desk or table when talking with someone.

When standing in conversation with someone, leaning against the wall or keeping hands in pockets is taken as a lack of respect.

Sitting in a manner that allows the sole of one's shoe to face another person is an insult.

Failure to shake hands when meeting someone or saying goodbye is considered rude. When a Western man is introduced to an Arab woman, it is the woman's choice whether to shake hands or not; she should be allowed to make the first move.

Casual dress at social events, many of which call for rather formal dress (a suit and tie for men, a dress and high heels for women), may be taken as a lack of respect for the hosts. There are, of course, some occasions on which casual dress is appropriate.

One who lights a cigarette in a group must be prepared to offer them to everyone.

Men stand when a woman enters a room; everyone stands when new guests arrive at a social gathering and when an elderly or high ranking person enters or leaves.

Men allow women to precede them through doorways and offer their seats to them if no others are available.

If guests admire something small and portable, an Arab may insist that it be taken as a gift. Guests need to be careful about expressing admiration for small, expensive possessions.

Gifts are given and accepted with both hands and are not opened in the presence of the donor.

In some social situations, especially in public places or when very tradition-bound people are present, Arabs consider it inappropriate for women to smoke or to drink alcoholic beverages.

When eating with Arabs, especially when taking food from communal dishes, the left hand is not used. (The left hand is considered unclean.)

At a restaurant, Arabs will almost always insist on paying, especially if there are not many people in the party or if it is a business-related occasion. Giving in graciously after a ritual gesture to pay and then returning the favor later is an appropriate response.

Arabs have definite ideas about what constitutes proper masculine and feminine behavior and appearance. They do not approve of long hair on men or mannish dress and comportment by women.

Family disagreements and disputes in front of others or within hearing of others are avoided by Arabs.

People should not be photographed without their permission.

Staring at other people is not usually considered rude or an invasion of privacy by Arabs (especially when the object is a fascinating foreigner). Moving away is the best defense.

When eating out with a large group of people where everyone is paying his share, it is best to let one person pay and reimburse him later. Arabs find the public calculation and division of a restaurant bill embarrassing.

Most Arabs do not like to touch or be in the presence of household animals, especially dogs. Pets are kept out of sight when Arab guests are present.

It is impossible, of course, to learn all the rules of a culture. The safest course of action is to imitate. In a social situation with Arabs, *never be the first one to do anything*! In some situations, such as in the presence of royalty, it is incorrect to cross your legs; in some situations, in the presence of royalty or a high-ranking older man, for instance, it is even incorrect to smoke.

7

The Social Structure

Arab society is structured into social classes, and individuals inherit the social class of their family. The governments of Libya and South Yemen are experimenting with classless societies, but these experiments have not yet affected basic attitudes.

Social Classes

There are three social classes in most Arab countries. The upper class is comprised of royalty (in some countries), large and influential families, and some wealthy people, depending on their family background. The middle class is comprised of government employees, military officers, teachers, and moderately prosperous merchants and landowners. The lower class is comprised of peasant farmers and the urban and village poor. Nomadic Bedouins do not really fit into any of these classes; they are mostly independent of society and are admired for their preservation of Arab traditions.

The relative degree of privilege among the classes, and the differences in their attitudes and way of life, vary from country to country. Some countries are wealthy and underpopulated, with a high percentage of their population in the privileged class; others are poor and overpopulated, with a high percentage of peasants and manual laborers.

There is usually very little tension among social classes. Arabs accept the social class into which they were born, and there is relatively little effort on the part of individuals to rise from one class to another. In any case it would be difficult for a person to change social class since it is determined almost entirely by family origin. A person can improve his status through his professional position and power, educational attainment, or acquired wealth, but his origins will be remembered. A family of the lower class could not really expect social acceptance in the upper class for two or three generations. Similarly, an upper-class family which squandered its wealth or influence would not be relegated to lower-class status for some time.

Foreign residents of Arab countries automatically accrue most of the status and privileges of the upper class. This is due to their professional standing, their level of education, and their income.

Image and Upper-Class Behavior

Certain kinds of behavior are expected of people of the upper class who wish to maintain their status and good public image. Some activities are not acceptable in public and if seen, cause shock and surprise.

If you know the basic norms of upper-class behavior, you will be free to decide the extent to which you are willing to conform. While you risk giving a negative impression by breaking a rule, doing so will not necessarily be offensive. You may simply be viewed as eccentric or as having poor judgment.

No upper-class person engages in manual labor in front of other people. Arabs are surprised when they see Westerners washing their cars or sweeping the sidewalk. While upper-class

Arabs may do some cleaning or polishing inside their homes, they do not do it in front of others.

A white-collar or desk job in an office is much desired by Arabs because of the status it confers. There is an enormous difference between working with the hands and working as a clerk. Any Arab who has a white-collar job will resent being asked to do something which he considers beneath his status. If, in an office situation, your requests are not being carried out, you may find that you have been asking a person to do something which is demeaning or threatening to his dignity. And not wishing to offend you, he would be hesitant to tell you.

An Egyptian interpreter in an American-managed hospital once told me that she was insulted when a Western doctor asked her to bring a glass of water. She felt that her dignity had been threatened and that she had been treated like the "tea boy" who took orders for drinks.

Manual work is fine if it can be classified as a hobby—for example, sewing, painting, or craftwork. Refinishing furniture might get by as a hobby, though it would probably raise eyebrows, but repairing cars is out. If you decide to paint the exterior of your house or refinish the floors yourself, expect to be talked about.

Upper-class Arabs are careful about their dress and appearance whenever they are in public because the way a person dresses indicates his wealth and social standing. Arab children are often dressed in expensive clothes, and women wear much jewelry, especially gold. The men are partial to expensive watches, cufflinks, pens, and cigarette lighters. Arabs feel that looking their best and dressing well are essential to their self-respect, and they are surprised when they see well-to-do people (i.e. foreigners) wearing casual or old clothes (faded jeans, a tattered T-shirt). Why would a person dress poorly when he or she can afford better?

Usually upper-class Arabs do not socialize with persons from other classes, at least not in each others' homes. They may enjoy cordial relations with the corner grocer and news-stand vendor, but they would not suggest a dinner or an evening's entertainment together. (A possible exception is a big occasion like the celebration of a wedding.)

When you plan social events, do not mix people from different social classes. You can invite anyone from any class to your home and the gesture is much appreciated, but to invite a company director and your local baker at the same time would embarrass both parties.

Dealing with Service People

If you live in an Arab country, you may well have one or more household servants, and you will soon establish a very personal relationship with them. Servants appreciate the kindness and consideration which they have come to expect from Westerners—"Please" and "Thank you" are never out of place. Frequently you may even work right alongside the servant. But you will notice that the relationship changes if Arab guests are present. Then the servant will want to do all the work alone so as not to tarnish your social image. If a glass of water is spilled, for example, you should call the servant to clean up, rather than be seen doing it yourself. Inviting your servant to join you and your guests at tea or at a meal would be inappropriate and very embarrassing for servant and guests.

Servants expect you to assume some responsibility for them; you may be asked to pay medical expenses and to help out financially in family emergencies. Give at least something as a token of concern, then ask around to find out how much is reasonable for the situation. If you feel that the expense is too high for you to cover completely, you can offer to lend the money and deduct it from the person's salary over a period of time. Be generous with surplus food and with household items or clothing you no longer need, and remember that extra money is expected on holidays.

Make the acquaintance of shopkeepers, doormen, and errand boys—most have delightful personalities and quickly become friends. Such acquaintances are best made by exchanging a few words of Arabic and showing them that you like and respect them.

If you become friendly with people who have relatively little money, watch the frequency of your social visits. They may be obliged to spend more than they can afford to receive you properly and the problem is far too embarrassing to discuss or even admit. It is enjoyable to visit villagers or the home of a taxi driver or shopkeeper, but if you plan to make it a habit, bring gifts with you or find other ways to compensate your hosts.

8

The Role of the Family

Arab society is built around the extended family system. Individuals feel a strong affiliation with all of their relatives— aunts, uncles, and cousins—not just with their immediate family. The degree to which all blood relationships are encompassed by a family unit varies among families, but most Arabs have over a hundred "fairly close" relatives.

Family Loyalty and Obligations

Family loyalty and obligations take precedence over loyalty to friends or the demands of a job. Relatives are expected to help each other, including giving financial assistance if necessary.

Family affiliation provides security. It assures one that he will never be entirely without resources, emotional or material. Only the most rash or foolhardy person would risk being censured or disowned by his family. Family support is indispensable in an unpredictable world; the family is a person's ultimate refuge.

Members of a family are expected to support each other in disputes with outsiders. Regardless of personal antipathy among relatives, they must defend each other's honor, counter criticism, and display group cohesion, if only for the sake of appearances. Internal family disputes rarely get to the point of open, public conflict.

Membership in a well-known and influential family ensures social acceptance and is often crucial to members in obtaining a good education, finding a good job, or succeeding in business. Arabs are very proud of their family connections and lineage.

The reputation of any member of a family group reflects on all of the other members. One person's indiscreet or ill-judged behavior can damage his relatives' pride, social influence and marriage opportunities. For this reason the family is the greatest source of pressure on an individual to conform to accepted behavior patterns. In Arab culture one is constantly reminded of his or her responsibility for upholding the honor of the family.

An employer must be understanding if an employee is late or absent because of family obligations. *It is unreasonable to expect an Arab employee to give priority to the demands of a job if they conflict with family duties.*

The description of Syrian society found in the book, *Syria, A Country Study,* is applicable to Arab societies in general:

> Syrians highly value family solidarity and, consequently, obedience of children to the wishes of their parents. Being a good family member includes automatic loyalty to kinsmen as well. Syrians employed in modern bureaucratic positions, such as government officials, therefore find impersonal impartiality difficult to attain because of a conflict with the deeply held value of family solidarity.
>
> There is no similarly ingrained feeling of duty toward a job, an employer, a co-worker, or even a friend. A widespread conviction exists that the only reliable people are one's kinsmen. An officeholder tends to select his kinsmen as fellow workers or subordinates because of a sense of responsibility for them and because of the feeling of trust between them. Commercial establishments are largely family operations staffed by the offspring and relatives of the owner. Cooperation among business firms

may be determined by the presence or absence of kinship ties between the heads of firms. When two young men become very close friends, they often enhance their relationship by accepting one another as "brothers," thus placing each in a position of special responsibility toward the other. There is no real basis for a close relationship except ties of kinship.[1]

A particularly revealing interview with two brothers working at the Helwan steel mill in Egypt and living with several other brothers included the following exchange:

> "I only earn £2 a month, said one brother . . . and this I give to my eldest brother. He takes it and buys food . . . if I need anything extra I ask him and he will get it for me."
>
> "Yes," the eldest said to us. "That's the way it is. I earn £25 a month and I support all of them . . . they have no work so I have to."
>
> "And what do you hope to gain?" we asked him.
>
> "Nothing," he answered. "Only I hope they will get on, achieve something with their lives. . . . I know that if I then fall on hard times, they will not forsake me."[2]

Relations Among Family Members

An Arab man is recognized as the head of his immediate family, and his role and influence are overt. His wife also has a clearly defined sphere of influence, but it exists largely "behind the scenes." An Arab woman does not always accord her husband the same deference in private which he receives in public.

In matters where opinions differ, much consultation and negotiation take place before decisions are made. If a compromise cannot be reached, however, the husband, father, or older men in the family prevail.

Status in a family is increased as a person grows older, and most families have patriarchs or matriarchs whose opinions are given considerable weight in family matters. Children are taught profound respect for adults, and this pattern of respect for age is pervasive in Arab society. It is common, for example, for adults to refrain from smoking in front of their parents or older relatives.

Responsibility for other members of the family rests heavily on older men in the extended family and on older sons in the immediate family. Children are their parents' "social security"—grown sons, in particular, are responsible for the support of their parents. In the absence of the father, brothers are responsible for their unmarried sisters.

Members of a family are very dependent on each other emotionally, and strong emotional ties continue throughout a person's life. Some people feel closer to their brothers and sisters and confide in them more than they do their spouses. Hall, in *The Hidden Dimension,* comments on this interdependence as it relates to the allocation of space in Arab homes:

> Arab spaces inside their upper middle-class homes are tremendous by our standards. They avoid partitions because Arabs do not like to be alone. The form of the home is such as to hold the family together inside a single protective shell, because Arabs are deeply involved with each other. Their personalities are intermingled and take nourishment from each other like the roots and soil. If one is not with people and actively involved in some way, one is deprived of life. An old Arab saying reflects this value: "Paradise without people should not be entered because it is Hell."[3]

In the traditional Arab family, the role of the mother and the father are quite different as they relate to their children. The mother is seen as a source of emotional support and steadfast loving kindness. She is patient, forgiving, and prone to indulge and spoil her children, especially her sons. The father is seen as a source of love, but may display affection less overtly; he is also the source of authority and punishment. Some Arab fathers feel that their status in the family is best maintained by cultivating awe and even a degree of fear in other members of the family.

In most Arab families the parents maintain very close contact with their own parents and with their brothers and sisters. For this reason, Arab children grow up experiencing constant interaction with older relatives, especially their grandparents, who often live in the same home. This contributes to the passing on of social values from one generation to another, as the influence of the older relatives is continually felt. Relatively few Arab teenagers and young adults rebel against family values and desires, certainly not to the extent common in Western societies. Even people who affect modern tastes in dress, reading material, and entertainment subscribe to prevailing social values and expect their own family lives to be very similar to that of their parents.

Marriage

Most Arabs still prefer family-arranged marriages. Even in some modern circles where changes in custom are taking place, the couples still seek family approval of the person they have chosen.

Arabs feel that because marriage is such a major decision it is considered prudent to leave it to the family's discretion rather than to choose someone solely on the basis of emotion or ideas of romance. In almost all Arab countries and social groups, however, the prospective bride and bridegroom have the opportunity to meet, visit, and become acquainted—and even to accept or reject a proposal of marriage. The degree to which the individuals are consulted will vary according to how traditional or modern the family is.

Among Moslem Arabs, especially in rural and nomadic communities, the preferred pattern of marriage is to a first or second cousin. Since an important part of a marriage arrangement is the investigation into the social and financial standing of the proposed candidates, it is reassuring to marry someone whose background, character, and financial position are well known. Marriages to cousins also ensure that money, in the form of a dowry or inheritance, stays within the family.

The practice of polygamy is becoming increasingly rare. It is practiced more among traditional groups and in conservative countries. It is an obligation as well as a privilege, since the Islamic religion requires a husband to provide for all of his wives equally. Polygamy is outlawed in Tunisia and Iraq and subject to court approval (if it might constitute an injustice to the first wife or if financial ability cannot be proven) in Morocco, Syria, Jordan, North Yemen, and South Yemen.[4]

In contrast to Western customs, Arab couples do not enter marriage with idealistic or romantic expectations. They are seeking companionship and love, but equally important, they want financial security, social status and children. These goals are realistic and are usually attained. Arab marriages are, on the whole, very stable and characterized by mutual respect. Having a happy family life is considered an important goal in the Arab World.

Divorce

Most Arab Christians belong to denominations which do not permit divorce. Among Moslems, divorce is permitted and carefully regulated by religious law.

Divorce is common enough that it does not carry a social stigma for the individuals involved. There is probably not as much personal pain associated with divorce if the marriage was arranged; obtaining a divorce is not an admission of mistaken judgment or an implied statement of personal failure as it is sometimes viewed in Western society. People who have been divorced are very eligible for remarriage.

A Moslem man may divorce his wife if he wishes, but he risks severe damage to his social image if he is arbitrary or hasty about his decision. A man can divorce his wife by pronouncing the formula of divorce ("I divorce you") in front of witnesses. If he says the formula once or twice, the couple can be reconciled; if he repeats it three times, it is binding. A woman has more difficulty in initiating divorce proceedings, but usually she is successful on grounds of childlessness, desertion, or non-support. A woman must go through court proceedings in order to divorce her husband. In Jordan, Syria, and Morocco, she may write into her marriage contract the right to initiate divorce.[5] Some Arab countries now require a man to go through court proceedings as well.

When a Moslem woman is divorced, her husband must pay a "divorce settlement," which is included in every marriage contract and is usually a very high sum. In addition she is entitled to financial support for herself for at least three months (a "waiting period" to determine that she is not pregnant) and more if she needs it, as well as support for her minor children.

Some Arab countries follow Islamic law entirely in matters of divorce; others have supplemented it. Laws pertaining to divorce have been widely discussed and changes are constantly being proposed. For example, the custody of children is theoretically determined by Islamic law. They are to stay with their mother to a certain age (approximately seven years for boys and nine years for girls, though it differs slightly among countries), and then they may go to their father. This shift is not always automatic, however, and may be ruled upon by a court or religious judge, according to the circumstances of the case.

Child-rearing Practices

Arabs dearly love children, and both men and women express that love openly. Arab children grow up surrounded by adoring relatives who share in child-rearing by feeding, caring for and even disciplining each other's children. Because so many people care for them and serve as authority figures and because the practice is so universal, Arabs are remarkably homogeneous in their experience of childhood. Arab children learn the *same* values in much the *same* way;

their upbringing is not as arbitrarily dependent on the approach of their particular parents as it is in Western societies.

In traditional Arab culture there has always been a marked preference for boys over girls because men contribute more to the family's influence in the community. Arab children are provided different role and personality models for men and women. Men are expected to be aggressive and decisive; women are expected to be more passive. The attitude toward boys and girls is starting to change now that women are being educated and becoming wage-earners. Many Arab couples practice birth control and limit the size of their families to two or three children, even if they are all girls.

Arab methods of disciplining children include shaming, comparison with others, and physical punishment (which is usually quick and not very severe). Adults usually do not reason with small children. They teach them to do things because "that is how it is done," or to avoid actions because "nobody does that—what would people say?" They are taught that conformity with an acceptable social image is the most important reason for modifying behavior. In a perceptive article, Hisham Sharabi and Mukhtar Ani discuss this type of behavioral conditioning:

> It is significant that an Arab child is conditioned to feel shame rather than guilt. He is made to feel ashamed because others *see* him as having acted wrongly, not because he inwardly *regrets* having done wrong and judges himself accordingly. In such conditioning, the capacity for self-criticism (self-condemnation) is not cultivated; instead, a reflex to social pressure and criticism is developed. Shame is formed by what the individual thinks others think of him, rather than by what he thinks of himself.[6]

Some educated or liberal-thinking Arabs find the pressure from the family to conform to rigid social standards to be oppressive. Much of what has been written on the subject of Arab character and personality development is extremely negative, particularly statements made by Arabs themselves.[7] Clearly many Arabs feel resentful of the requirements imposed by their families and by society and believe that conformity leads to the development of undesirable personal traits. Hamady makes this point emphatically:

> He [the Arab] is tied hand and foot by the demands and interference of his group. He is not left alone to do what he pleases. His duties, if not fulfilled, are exacted from him. Advice is given even when not asked for. . . . He may not make decisions for himself without consulting his near relatives and the senior members of his group.[8]

Most Arabs feel that while their childhood was, in many ways, a time of stringent demands, it was also a time of indulgence and openly-expressed love, especially from their mother. Failure to conform is punished, but methods of discipline are not harsh. Arab parents are shocked by some Western methods of child discipline such as the denial of food (being sent to bed without dinner) or solitary confinement (being sent to a room alone).

In Arab culture, the most important requirement for a "good" child is respectful behavior in front of adults. Children must greet adults with a handshake, stay to converse for a few minutes if asked, and refrain from interrupting or talking back. Children often help to serve guests and thus learn the requirements of hospitality early. Westerners who want their children to make a good impression on Arab guests might wish to keep this custom in mind.

Among Arabs it is an extremely important responsibility to bring children up so that they will reflect well on the family. It is an insult to accuse someone of not being "well-raised." A child's character and success in life reflects directly on its parents. Arabs tend to give parents much of the credit for their children's successes and much of the blame for their failures. Parents readily make sacrifices for their children's welfare; they expect these efforts to be acknowledged and their parental influence to continue throughout the child's life.

Many Western parents begin training their children at an early age to become independent and self-reliant. They give the children token jobs and regular allowance money and frequently encourage them to make their own decisions. This training helps children avoid being dependent on their parents after they have reached adulthood.

Arab parents, on the other hand, welcome their children's dependence. Mothers especially try to keep their children tied to them emotionally. Young people continue to live at home until they are married and then, at least in traditional families, young married couples live with the husband's parents. It is customary for the parents of a newly-married couple to furnish the couple's home entirely and to continue to help them financially.

Talking about Your Family

Given this emphasis on family background and honor, you may want to carefully consider the impression you will make when giving information to Arabs about your family relationships. Saying the wrong thing can affect your image and status.

Arabs are very surprised if someone talks about poverty and disadvantages experienced in early life. Rather than admiring his success in overcoming such circumstances, they wonder why anyone would admit to humble origins when it need not be known.

If your father held a low-status job, if you have relatives, especially female relatives, who are "black sheep" and have done disgraceful things, or if you have elderly relatives in a nursing home (which Arabs find shocking), there is nothing to be gained by talking about it. If you dislike your parents or any close relatives, keep it to yourself. On the other hand, if you are from a prominent family or are related to a well-known person, letting people know it can work to your advantage.

In sum, if you do not have positive things to say about your family, things that will incline Arabs to admiration, it is best to talk about something else.

9

9

Religion and Society

Arabs identify strongly with their religious groups, whether they are Moslem or Christian and whether they follow religious observances or not. A foreigner must be aware of the pervasive role of religion in Arab life in order to avoid causing offense by injudicious statements or actions.

Religious Affiliation

Religious affiliation is essential for every person in Arab society—there is no place for an atheist or an agnostic. If you have no religious affiliation or are an atheist, it is best to keep it to yourself. Shock and amazement would be the reaction of most Arabs, along with a loss of respect for you. Arabs place great value on piety and respect anyone who sincerely practices his religion, no matter what religion it is.

Religious Practices

An Arab's religion affects his whole way of life on a daily basis. Religion is taught in the schools, the language is full of religious expressions, and people practice their religion openly, almost obtrusively, expressing it in numerous ways: decorations on cars and in homes; jewelry in the form of gold crosses, miniature Korans or pendants inscribed with Koranic verses; religious names.

Moslems say the Koranic formula, "In the name of God, the Merciful, the Compassionate" (Bismillah Ar-Rahman Ar-Raheem), whenever they are setting out on a trip, about to undertake a dangerous task, or beginning a speech. This formula is printed at the top of business letterheads and included at the beginning of reports and personal letters—it even appears on business receipts!

For both Moslems and Christians, marriage and divorce are controlled by religious law. In some countries there is no such thing as a civil marriage; it must be performed by a religious official. For Moslems, inheritance is also controlled by religious law. In conservative countries religious law partially determines methods of criminal punishment.

The practice of "Islamic banking" is gaining in popularity. The Islamic religion forbids lending money at a fixed rate of interest, viewing it as an unfair and exploitative use of money. Islamic banks, therefore, place investors' money in "shared risk" partnership accounts, with rates of return varying according to profits (or losses) on investments. In 1984 there were about thirty such banks in Jordan, Egypt, Sudan, Kuwait, Bahrain, the Gulf States and Saudi Arabia.

Marriage across religious lines is rare although the Islamic religion permits a Moslem man to marry a Jewish or Christian woman without requiring that his wife convert. A Moslem woman, however, must marry a Moslem man. In this way the children are assured of being Moslem; children are considered to have the religion of their father.

Never make critical remarks about any religious practice. *In Arab culture all religions and their practices are treated with respect.*

If you are a Christian foreigner and ask Christian Arabs about accompanying them to church services, they will be very pleased. You are not welcome at Islamic religious services, however, and should not enter a mosque until you have checked whether it is permitted, which varies from country to country and even from mosque to mosque.

The Religion of Islam

To understand Arab culture it is essential to become familiar with the outlines of Islamic history and doctrine. If you do, you will gain insights rare among Westerners and will be greatly appreciated by Arabs for the efforts you have made.

The Islamic religion had its origin in northern Arabia in the Seventh Century, A.D. The doctrines of Islam are based on revelations from God to His last prophet, Mohamed, over a period of twenty-two years. The revelations were preserved and incorporated into the holy book of the Moslems, the Koran.

The God Moslems worship is the same God Jews and Christians worship ("Allah" is simply the Arabic word for "God").

The Koran contains doctrines which guide Moslems to correct behavior so that they will find salvation on the Day of Judgment, narrative stories illustrating God's benevolence and power, and social regulations for the Moslem community. It is the single most important guiding force for Moslems and touches on virtually every aspect of their lives.

The word "Islam" means "submission to the will of God," and a "Moslem" (also spelled "Muslim," which is closer to the Arabic pronunciation) is "one who submits." The doctrines of the Islamic religion are viewed as a summation and completion of previous revelations to Jewish and Christian prophets. Islam shares many doctrines with Judaism and Christianity, and Jews and Christians are known as "People of the Book."

Shortly after the advent of Islam, the Arabs began an energetic conquest of surrounding territory and eventually expanded their empire from Spain to India. The widespread conversion to Islam by the people in the Middle East and North Africa accounts for the fact that today over 90% of the Arabs are Moslems.

Most Moslem Arabs are Sunni (also called "orthodox"), but sizable numbers of Shiite Moslems are found in Lebanon, Iraq, and the Arabian Gulf. The separation of the Moslems into two groups stems from a dispute over the proper succession of authority (the "caliphate") after the death of the Prophet Mohamed. Sunnis and Shiites differ today in some of their religious practices and emphasis on certain doctrines, but both groups recognize each other as Moslems.

Moslem society is governed by the Sharia, or Islamic law, which is based on the Koran and the Sunnah. The Sunnah is the description of the acts and sayings of the Prophet and incorporates the Hadith (traditions of the Prophet). Islamic jurists also use Ijma' (consensus) and Qiyas (reasoning by analogy) when interpreting and applying Islamic law.

The application of Islamic law differs by country and local interpretation of the Koran and Sharia law. Some countries follow it almost exclusively in domestic and criminal law (Saudi Arabia, Libya, Sudan) but most have modified or supplemented it. Islamic jurists are faced with new issues on which there has not been final agreement; birth control, for instance, which is permitted in most Islamic countries, is openly promoted by some and discouraged by others. Pakistan (a Moslem, non-Arab country) outlawed birth control on the basis of religious principles.

The basic tenets of the Islamic faith are the five "pillars" (primary obligations) of Islam:

The declaration of faith ("There is no God but God and Mohamed is the Messenger [Prophet] of God"). The recitation of this declaration with sincere intention in front of two male Moslem witnesses is sufficient for a person to become a Moslem. (Moslems will welcome your acknowledgment of belief in God and His control over men's lives.)

Prayer, five times daily.   The five prayers are Dawn, Noon, Afternoon, Sunset and Night, and their times differ slightly every day. Moslems are reminded of prayer through a "prayer call" broadcast from the minaret of a mosque. A Moslem prays facing in the direction of the Kaaba in Mecca. Prayer is regulated by ritual purification beforehand and a predetermined number of prostrations and recitations, depending on the time of day. Moslems may pray in a mosque, in their home or office, or in public places. (Avoid staring at, walking in front of, or interrupting a person during prayer.)

Giving alms (charity) to the needy.   Moslems are required to give a certain amount of their income for the welfare of the community in general and the poor in particular. (If you are asked for alms by a beggar, it is best to give a token amount. Even if you give nothing, avoid saying the word "No," which is very rude. Say instead "Allah ya'teek" ("God give you"); at least you have given the person a blessing.

Fasting during the month of Ramadan.   Ramadan is the ninth month of the Islamic lunar calendar. During Ramadan, Moslems do not eat, drink, or smoke between sunrise and sunset. The purpose of fasting is to experience hunger and deprivation and to perform an act of self-discipline, humility, and faith. The Ramadan fast is not required of persons whose health may be endangered (travelers are also excused); however, anyone who is excused must make up fast days later when health permits. In most communities, Ramadan brings with it a holiday atmosphere, as people gather with family and friends to break the fast at elaborate meals. Work hours are shortened, shops change their opening hours, and most activities take place in the early morning or late at night.

Be considerate of people who are fasting during Ramadan by refraining from eating, drinking, or smoking in public places during the fasting hours. To express good wishes to someone before or during Ramadan, you say "Ramadan Kareem" ("Gracious Ramadan"), to which the response is "Allahu Akram" ("God is more gracious").

Performing a pilgrimage to Mecca at least once during one's lifetime if it is not a financial hardship. The pilgrimage, or "Hajj," is the peak of religious experience for many Moslems. It takes place in the twelfth month of the Islamic year, and is an impressive gathering of Moslems from all over the world. The Hajj consists of several separate activities which are carried out at different sites in the Mecca area, over a period of six days. Pilgrims, men and women, wear white garments to symbolize their state of purity and their equality in the sight of God. The Hajj period concludes with a holiday on which it is customary for families who can afford it to sacrifice a sheep and share a portion with the poor.

When someone is departing for the pilgrimage, the appropriate blessing is "Hajj Mabroor" ("Reverent Pilgrimage"). When someone returns, you offer congratulations and add the title "Hajj" ("Hajja" for a woman) to the person's name (except in Saudi Arabia, where the Hajj title is not used).

The Koran and the Bible

Much of the content of the Koran is similar to the teachings and stories found in the Old and New Testaments of the Bible. Islamic doctrine accepts the previous revelations to Biblical prophets as valid, but states, as the Bible does, that the people continually strayed from these teachings. Correct guidance had to be repeated through different prophets, one after the other. By the Seventh Century, doctrines and practices again had to be corrected through the revelations to Mohamed, who is known as the last, or "seal," of the prophets.

The Koran is divided into 114 chapters, arranged in reverse order of length, i.e., longest to shortest (with a few exceptions). The chapters are *not* in chronological order, although they are identified as to whether they were revealed in Mecca (earlier), or Medina (later). Each chapter (Surah) is comprised of verses (Ayat). If you decide to read the Koran in translation, it is a good idea to obtain a list of the chapters in chronological order and read through them in that order so that the development of thought and teachings becomes clear.[1]

Most of the chapters in the Koran are in cadenced, rhymed verse, while some (particularly the later Medinan ones) are in prose. The sustained rhythm of the recited Koran, combined with the beauty of its content, accounts for its great esthetic and poetic effect when heard in Arabic. The Koran is considered the epitome of Arabic writing style, and when it is recited aloud, it can move listeners to tears. The excellence of the Koran is taken as one proof of its divine origin—no human being could expect to imitate it successfully.

The Koran has several notable characteristics. Those most often cited are: it is inimitable, it is eternal (it always existed, but was not manifested until the seventh century), and it is in Arabic (the Arabic version is the direct Word of God, so translations of the Koran into other languages are not used for prayer).

It is very common for Moslems to memorize the Koran, or large portions of it; a person who can recite the Koran is called a "Hafiz." Reading and reciting the Koran was once the traditional form of education, and often the only education many people received. In most schools today memorization of Koranic passages is included in the curriculum. The word "Koran" means "Recitation" in Arabic.

The Koran and the Bible have much in common:

–the necessity of faith.

–reward for good actions and punishment for evil actions on the Day of Judgment.

–the concept of Heaven (Paradise) and Hell.

–the existence of angels who communicate between God and man.

–the existence of Satan ("Shaytan" in Arabic).

—the recognition of numerous prophets. The Koran recognizes eighteen Old Testament figures as prophets (among them Adam, Noah, Abraham, Ishmael, Isaac, Jacob, Moses, Joseph, Job), three New Testament figures (Zachariah, John the Baptist, and Jesus), and mentions four prophets who do not appear in the Bible. Of all these prophets, five are considered the most important. In order of chronology these are: Noah, Abraham, Moses, Jesus, and Mohamed.

—the prohibition of the consumption of pork and the flesh of animals not slaughtered in a ritual manner. This is very similar to kosher dietary law in the Old Testament.

—the teaching that Jesus was born of a virgin. Mary is called "Miriam" in Arabic.

—the teaching that Jesus worked miracles, including curing the sick and raising the dead.

There are some notable differences between the Koran and the Bible as well:

—Islam does not recognize the concept of intercession between God and man. All prayers must be made to God directly. For this reason Jesus is recognized as one of the most important prophets, but the Christian concept of his intercession for man's sins is not accepted.

—Islam teaches that Jesus was not crucified; instead, a person who looked like him was miraculously substituted in his place on the cross. God would not allow such an event to happen to one of His prophets.

—Islam does not accept the doctrine of Jesus' resurrection and divinity.

—Islam is uncompromisingly monotheistic and rejects the Christian concept of the Trinity.

Some of the Biblical stories which are re-told in the Koran (in a shortened version) include:

–the story of the Creation.

–the story of Adam and Eve.

–the story of Cain and Abel.

–the story of Noah and the Flood.

–the story of the covenant of Abraham and his willingness to sacrifice his son as a test of faith. Islam holds that he was ordered to sacrifice Ishmael, whereas the Bible states that it was Isaac. Abraham is recognized as the ancestor of the Arabs through Ishmael.

–the story of Lot and the destruction of the evil cities.

–the story of Joseph (told in more detail).

–the story of Moses and the Exodus from Egypt.

–the story of David and Goliath.

–the story of Solomon and the Queen of Sheba.

–the story of the afflictions of Job.

–the story of the birth of Jesus. In the Koranic version, Jesus was born at the foot of a palm tree in the desert and saved his unmarried mother from scorn when, as an infant, he spoke up in her defense and declared himself a prophet, saying ". . . Peace be upon me, the day I was born, and the day I die, and the day I am raised up alive" (referring to his resurrection on the Day of Judgment). This is a miracle of Jesus not recorded in the Bible.

Moslems feel an affinity with the Jewish and Christian religions, and they find it unfortunate that so few Westerners understand how similar the Islamic religion is to their own. Islam is a continuation of the other two religions, and Moslems view it as the one true faith.

Passages from the Koran

Selected passages from the Koran are presented here to give an idea of the tone and content the book (from *The Koran Interpreted,* by A.J. Arberry).

CHAPTER 1   THE OPENING

In the Name of God, the Merciful, the Compassionate.

Praise belongs to God, the Lord of all Being
the All-merciful, the All-compassionate
the Master of the Day of Doom.

Thee only we serve; to Thee alone we pray for succour.
Guide us in the straight path,
the path of those whom Thou hast blessed,
not of those against whom Thou art wrathful,
nor of those who are astray.

CHAPTER 5   THE TABLE

(Titles of chapters refer to key words in that chapter, not to content.)

(Verse 3)

Today the unbelievers have despaired of
your religion; therefore fear them not,
but fear you Me.
Today I have perfected your religion
for you, and I have completed My blessing
upon you, and I have approved Islam for
your religion.

(Verse 120)

To God belongs the kingdom of the heavens
and of the earth, and all that is in them,
and He is powerful over everything.

CHAPTER 93   THE FORENOON

(This chapter begins with an oath, which is common in the Koran.)

In the Name of God, the Merciful, the Compassionate.

By the white forenoon
and the brooding night!
Thy Lord has neither forsaken thee nor hates thee
and the Last shall be better for thee than the First.
Thy Lord shall give thee, and thou shalt be satisfied.

Did He not find thee an orphan, and shelter thee?
Did He not find thee erring, and guide thee?
Did He not find thee needy, and suffice thee?

As for the orphan, do not oppress him,
and as for the beggar, scold him not;
and as for thy Lord's blessing, declare it.

10

١٠

Communicating with Arabs

Even if you never learn Arabic, you will need to know something about the language and how it is used.

Arabic is the native language of 150 million people and the official language of twenty countries. In 1973 it was named the sixth official language of the United Nations and is tied with Bengali as the fourth most widely-spoken language in the world.[1]

Arabic originated as one of the "northern Semitic" languages. The only other Semitic languages still in wide use today are Hebrew (revived as a spoken language only in this century) and Amharic (Ethiopian), which is from the "southern Semitic" branch. There are still a few speakers of the northern Semitic languages (Aramaic, Syriac and Chaldean) in Lebanon, Syria and Iraq.

Many English words have been borrowed from Arabic, the most easily recognizable being those which begin with "al" (the Arabic word for "the"), such as *algebra, alchemy, alcove, alcohol,* and *alkali.* Many pertain to mathematics and the sciences; medieval European scholars drew heavily on Arabic source materials in these fields. Other Arabic words include *cipher, azimuth, algorithm,* and *almanac.* Some foods which originated in the East brought their Arabic names West with them—*coffee, sherbet, sesame, apricot, ginger, saffron, carob.*

Varieties of Arabic

Spoken Arabic in all its forms is very different from written Arabic. The written version is Classical Arabic, the language which was in use in the seventh century, A.D., in the Hijaz area of Arabia. It is the rich, poetic language of the Koran which has persisted as the written language of all Arabic-speaking peoples since that time. Classical Arabic, which has evolved into Modern Standard Arabic to accommodate new words and usages, is sacred to the Arabs, esthetically pleasing, and far more grammatically complex than the spoken or "colloquial" dialects.

The spoken languages are Formal Spoken Arabic and Colloquial Arabic, which includes many dialects and sub-dialects. Some of them differ from each other as much as Spanish differs from Italian or the Scandinavian languages differ from each other, but they are all recognized as Arabic. When Arabic spread throughout the Middle East and North Africa with the Arab conquests, it mixed with and assimilated local languages, spawning the dialects which are spoken today.

An overview of Arabic language usage now reveals the following:

1. *Classical (Modern Standard) Arabic.* Classical Arabic is used for all writing and for formal discussions, speeches, and news broadcasts but not for ordinary conversation. It is the same in all Arab countries, except for occasional variations in vocabulary which are regional or specialized.

2. *Colloquial Arabic (dialects).* Colloquial Arabic is used for everyday spoken communication but not for writing, except sometimes in very informal correspondence, in film or play scripts, or as slang in cartoons and the like.

3. *Formal Spoken Arabic.* Formal Spoken Arabic is improvised, consisting principally of using Classical Arabic terminology within the structure of the local dialect and is used by educated persons when they converse with Arabs whose dialect is very different from their own.

The Superiority of Arabic

Arabs are secure in the knowledge that their language is superior to all others. This attitude about one's own language is held by many people in the world, but in the case of the Arabs, they can point to several factors as proof of their assertion.

Most important, when the Koran came directly from God, Arabic was the medium *chosen* for His message. Its use was not an accident. Arabic is also extremely difficult and complex grammatically, which is viewed as another sign of superiority. Its structure lends itself to rhythm and rhyme, so it is pleasing to listen to when recited aloud. It has an unusually large vocabulary and the grammar allows for the easy coining of new words, so that borrowing from other languages is less common in Arabic than in many other languages. In other words, Arabic is richer than others, or so it is argued.

While most Westerners feel an affection for their native language, the pride and love which Arabs feel for Arabic is much more intense. The Arabic language is one of their greatest cultural treasures and achievements.

The Prestige of Classical Arabic

The reverence for Arabic pertains only to Classical Arabic, which is what Arabs mean by the phrase, "the Arabic Language." This was illustrated by the comment of an Egyptian village headman who was explaining why he considered the village school to be important. "For one thing," he said, "that's where the children go to learn Arabic."

The Arabic dialects have no prestige. Some people go so far as to suggest that they have "no grammar" and are not worthy of serious study. Committees of scholars have coined new words and tried to impose conventional usages to partially replace the dialects, but they have had no more success than language-regulatory groups in other countries.

A good command of Classical Arabic is highly admired in the Arab culture because it is difficult to attain. Few people other than scholars and specialists in Arabic have enough confidence to speak extemporaneously in Classical Arabic or to defend their written style.

To become truly literate in Arabic requires more years of study than are required for English literacy. The student must learn new words in Classical Arabic (more than 50% of the words are different from the local dialect in some countries)[2] and a whole new grammar, including case endings and new verb forms. The literacy problem in the Arab World stems significantly from the difficulty of Classical Arabic. Even people who can read and write are still "functionally illiterate" (unable to use the written language for more than rudimentary needs, such as signing one's name or reading signs) if they have had only five or six years of schooling.

From time to time Arab scholars have suggested that Classical Arabic be replaced by written dialects in order to facilitate education and literacy. This idea has been repeatedly and emphatically denounced by the large majority of Arabs and has almost no chance of acceptance in the foreseeable future. The most serious objection is that it is the language of the Koran. Another argument is that if Classical Arabic were supplanted by the dialects, the entire body of Arabic literature and poetry would become unattainable, and, if translated into a dialect, it would lose much of its beauty.

But there is a political argument too. Classical Arabic is a cultural force which unites all Arabs. To discard it, many fear, would lead to a linguistic fragmentation which would exacerbate the tendencies toward political and psychological fragmentation already present.

Eloquence of Speech

Eloquence is emphasized and admired in the Arab World far more than in the West, which accounts for the "flowery" prose in Arabic, both in written and spoken form. *Instead of viewing rhetoric in a disparaging way, as Westerners often do, Arabs admire it.* The ability to speak eloquently is a sign of education and refinement.

Foreign observers frequently comment on long-winded political speeches and the repetition of phrases and themes in Arabic, failing to understand that the speaker's style of delivery and command of the language appeal to the listeners as much as the message itself. Exaggerations, threats, promises, and nationalistic slogans are meant more for momentary effect than as statements of policy or belief, yet foreigners too often take them literally, especially when encountered in the cold light of a foreign language translation.

In the Arab World how you say something is as important as what you have to say.

Eloquence is a clue to the popular appeal of some nationalistic leaders whose words are far more compelling than their deeds. Much of the personal charisma attributed to them is due in large part to their ability to speak in well-phrased, rhetorical Arabic. This was true of the late Gamal Abdel Nasser, for example, and is true of Muammar Qaddhafi today.

Arabs devote considerable effort to using their language creatively and effectively. As Leslie J. McLoughlin, an Arabic specialist, says:

> Westerners are not in everyday speech given, as Arabs are, to quoting poetry, ancient proverbs and extracts from holy books. Nor are they wont to exchange fulsome greetings. . . . Perhaps the greatest difference between the Levantine approach to language and that of westerners is that Levantines, like most Arabs, take pleasure in using language for its own sake. The *sahra* (or evening entertainment) may well take the form of talk alone, but talk of a kind forgotten in the west except in isolated communities such as Irish villages or Swiss mountain communities—talk not merely comical, tragical, historical/pastoral, etc. but talk ranging over poetry, story-telling, anecdotes, jokes, word-games, singing and acting.[3]

Speech Mannerisms

It is a difficult task to make yourself completely understood by another person under the best of circumstances. It is more difficult still if you each have dramatically different ways of expressing yourself. Such is the problem between Westerners and Arabs, which often results in misunderstanding, leaving both parties feeling bewildered or deceived.

Arabs talk a lot, repeat themselves, shout when excited, and make extensive use of gestures. They punctuate their conversations with oaths (such as "I swear by God") to emphasize what they say, and they exaggerate for effect. Foreigners sometimes wonder if they are involved in a discussion or an argument.

If you speak softly and make your statements only once, Arabs may wonder if you really mean what you are saying. People will ask, "Do you really mean that?" or "Is that true?"—not that they do not believe you, but they need repetition and a few emphatic "yeses" to be reassured.

Arabs have a great tolerance for noise and interference during discussions; often several people speak at once (each trying to outshout the other) and intersperse their statements with table-pounding and threatening (or playful) gestures, while being coached by bystanders. Businessmen interrupt meetings to greet callers, answer the telephone and sign papers brought in by clerks. A foreigner may feel that he can be heard only if he insists on the pre-condition of being allowed to speak without interruption.

Loudness of speech is mainly for dramatic effect and in most cases should not be taken as an indication of how definite the speaker feels about what he is saying.

In a taxi in Cairo once, my driver was shouting and complaining and gesticulating wildly to other drivers as he worked his way through the crowded streets. In the midst of all this action, he turned around, laughed and winked. "You know," he said, "sometimes I really enjoy this!"

Some situations absolutely demand emotion and drama. In Baghdad I was in a taxi when it was hit from the rear. Both drivers leapt out of their cars and began shouting at each other. After waiting ten minutes, while a crowd gathered, I decided to pay the fare and leave. I pushed through the crowd and got the driver's attention. He broke off the argument, politely told me that there was nothing to pay, and then resumed the argument at full voice.

Loud and boisterous behavior is more frequent, of course, among people of approximately the same age and social status who know each other well. It occurs mostly in social situations, less often in business meetings. It is not acceptable when dealing with elders or social superiors, in which case polite deference is required. Bedouins and the Arabs of Saudi Arabia and the Gulf tend to be more reserved and soft-spoken, at least in more or less formal discussions. *In almost every respect protocol is stricter in the Arabian Peninsula.*

The Power of Words

To the Arab way of thinking (consciously or subconsciously), words have *power;* they can affect events. Arab conversation is peppered with blessings, which are like little prayers for good fortune, intended to help keep things going well. At the same time *swearing and the use of curses and obscenities are very offensive to Arabs.* If words have power and can affect events, it is feared that curses may bring misfortune just by being uttered.

The liberal use of blessings also demonstrates that the speaker holds no envy toward a person or object; in other words, that he does not cast an "evil eye" toward something. Belief in the evil eye (often just called "the eye") is common and it is feared or acknowledged to some extent by most Arabs, although less by the better educated.

It is widely believed among Arabs that a person or object can be harmed if someone looks at it (even unconsciously) with envy—with an "evil eye." The harm may be prevented, however, by offering blessings or statements of good will. Even foreigners who do not know about the evil eye may be suspected of giving it. When a Jordanian proudly showed a British friend his new car, the Britisher said, "It's beautiful! I wish I could afford a car like that!" Two weeks later the Jordanian had a serious car accident. When his British friend paid him a call, the Jordanian received him coolly and their friendship never revived. The Britisher now believes that it was his inadvertent expression of apparent envy that destroyed the friendship.

Some examples of things you can say (in English as well as Arabic) are listed in Appendix A.

Euphemisms

Arabs are uncomfortable discussing illness, disaster or death. This trait illustrates how the power of words affects Arab speech and behavior. *A careless reference to bad events can lead to misfortune or make a bad situation worse.* Arabs avoid such references as much as possible and use euphemisms instead.

Euphemisms serve as substitutes and a foreigner needs to learn the "code" in order to understand what is really meant. For example, instead of saying that someone is sick, an Arab may describe him as "a little tired." They avoid a word like "cancer" ("He has 'it', " or "He has 'the disease'") and often wait until an illness is over before telling others about it, even relatives. Arabs do not speak easily about death and sometimes avoid telling others about a death for some time, and even then they will phrase it euphemistically.

Some years back I was visiting the owner of an Egyptian country estate when two men came in supporting a third man who had collapsed in the field. The landlord quickly telephoned the local health unit. He got through just as the man slipped from his chair and appeared to be having a heart attack. "Ambulance!," he screamed, "Send me an ambulance! I have a man here who's . . . a little tired!"

I also had an amusing experience listening to an American life-insurance salesman discuss a policy with an Arab. "Now if you should be killed," he began, "or become paralyzed, or blind, or lose a limb. . . ." The conversation ended rather quickly; the Arab decided he did not want to hear about that policy!

In technical situations, of course, where specificity is required (doctor to patient; commander to soldier), explicit language is used.

The Written Word

The Arabs have considerable respect for the written as well as the spoken word. Some pious people feel that anything written in Arabic should be burned when no longer needed (such as newspapers), or at least not left on the street to be walked on or used to wrap things because the name of God probably appears somewhere. Decorations using Arabic calligraphy, Koranic quotations and the name "Allah" are never used on floors. They are often seen, however, in framed pictures or painted on walls. If you buy anything decorated with Arabic calligraphy, ask what it means; you could offend Arabs by the careless handling of an item decorated with a religious quotation.

If you own an Arabic Koran, you must handle it with respect. It should be placed flat on a table or in its own area on a shelf, not wedged in with many other books. Best of all, keep it in a velvet box or display it on an X-shaped wooden stand, both made for this purpose. Under no circumstances should anything (an ashtray, another book) be placed on top of the Koran. Never set the Koran on the floor.

Written blessings and Koranic verses are effective in assuring safety and preventing the evil eye, so they are seen all over the Arab World. Blessings are painted on cars and trucks and engraved on jewelry. You will see religious phrases in combination with the color blue, drawings of eyes, or open palmprints, all of which appear on amulets against the evil eye.

Proverbs

Arabs make abundant use of proverbs, of which they have hundreds. Many are in the form of rhymes or couplets. A person's knowledge of proverbs and when to use them enhances his image by demonstrating his wisdom and insight.

Here is a selection of Arab proverbs which help illuminate their outlook on life. Proverbs frequently refer to family and relatives, patience and defeatism, poverty and social inequality, fate and luck.

—Support your brother, whether he is the tyrant or the tyrannized.

—The knife of the family does not cut.
  (If you are harmed by a relative, don't take offense.)

—You are like a tree, giving your shade to the outside.
  (You should give more attention to your own family.)

—One hand alone does not clap.
  (Cooperation is essential.)

—The hand of God is with the group.
  (There is strength in unity.)

—The young goose is a good swimmer.
  (Like father, like son.)

—Older than you by a day, wiser than you by a year.
  (Respect older people and their advice.)

—The eye cannot rise above the eyebrow.
  (Be satisfied with your station in life.)

—The world is changeable, one day honey and the next day onions.

–Every sun has to set.
  (Fame and fortune may be fleeting.)

–Seven trades but no luck.
  (Even if a person is qualifed in many trades, because of bad luck he may not find work.)

–It's all fate and chance.

–If a rich man ate a snake, they would say it was because of his wisdom; if a poor man ate it, they would say it was because of his stupidity.

–Your tongue is like a horse—if you take care of it, it takes care of you; if you treat it badly, it treats you badly.

–The dogs may bark but the caravan moves on.
  (A person should rise above petty criticism.)

–Patience is beautiful.

–A concealed sin is two-thirds forgiven.

–The slave does the thinking and the lord carries it out.
  (Man proposes and God disposes.)

–Bounties are from God.
  (All good things come from God.)

  And finally, my very favorite:

–The monkey in the eyes of his mother is a gazelle.
  (There's nothing quite like motherly love!)

Conclusion

The more you socialize and interact with Arabs, the sooner you will abandon stereotyped impressions you may have brought with you. Individuals behave differently, but patterns emerge if you look for them. Soon you will be able to understand and even predict actions and reactions, some of which may be different from what you expected. Your task is to become aware of how and why things happen in order to feel comfortable with new social patterns as soon as possible.

Arab culture is complex but not unfathomable or totally exotic; many people find it similar to life in the Mediterranean area and Latin America. Arabs are demonstrative, emotional, and full of zest for life, while at the same time bound by stringent rules and expectations. Westerners need not feel obliged to imitate Arabs in order to be accepted. All that is necessary for harmonious relations is to be non-judgmental and to avoid any actions which are insulting or shocking. Westerners, especially North Americans, are accustomed to being open and "up front" with beliefs and feelings, particularly since the 1960's. This forthrightness needs to be tempered when operating in the tradition-bound culture of the Middle East.

Arabs are accustomed to dealing with foreigners and expect them to behave and dress differently and to have different ideas. Foreigners are forgiven a great deal—even conservative people make allowances, particularly when they know your motives are good. The essential thing is to make a sincere, well-meaning effort to adapt and understand. This attitude is readily apparent and will go a long way in helping you form comfortable work relations and friendships. Perhaps you may even get on good enough terms with an Arab friend to ask for constructive criticism from time to time. If you do, tactful hints will be offered—listen for them.

Most Arabs are genuinely interested in foreigners and enjoy talking to and developing friendships with them. But their attitude toward Westerners is a mixture of awe, good will, and resentment. They admire Westerners' education and expertise, and most of them have heard favorable reports from others who have visited Western countries. Many Arabs express the hope that they can visit or study in the West. In some countries, travel and emigration to Western countries are popular.

At the same time Arabs feel that Western societies are too liberal in many ways and that Westerners are not careful enough about their personal and social appearance. Arabs are sensitive to any display of arrogance by Westerners and to implied criticisms. They have a great deal of pride, and are easily hurt. They also frequently disapprove of and resent Western policies in the Arab World.

Moving to an Arab country or interacting with Arabs need not be a source of anxiety. If you use common sense, make an effort to be considerate, and apply your knowledge of Arab customs and traditions, it will be easy to conduct yourself in a way which reflects creditably on your background and home country and at the same time to have a rich and rewarding experience.

Appendix A
The Arabic Language

Learning Arabic is, of course, indispensable for gaining a real insight into the society and culture. If you intend to study Arabic, you should choose the variety which is most useful for your own needs.

Arabs associate foreign learners of Arabic with scholars, who, in the past, have tended to concentrate on Classical Arabic; so if you ask an Arab to give you lessons in Arabic, he will usually want to start with the alphabet and emphasize reading. If your interest is mainly in learning spoken Arabic, you will have to make that clear from the outset.

When you speak Arabic, you will find that your use of even the simplest phrases, no matter how poorly pronounced, produces an immediate smile and comment of appreciation. I have had literally hundreds of occasions on which my willingness to converse in Arabic led to a delightful experience. One example occurred in 1974, when I was shopping in a small town in Lebanon and spent about half an hour chatting with the owner of one of the shops. When I was about to leave, he insisted on giving me a small brass camel, "because you speak Arabic."

Arabs are flattered by your efforts to learn their language (although they are convinced that no foreigner can ever master it), and they will do everything to encourage you. Even just a little Arabic is a useful tool for forming friendships and demonstrating good will.

Arabic Dialects

The Arabic dialects fall into five geographical categories:

Category	Dialects	Native or Other Language Influence
1. North African (Western Arabic)	Moroccan Algerian Tunisian Libyan Mauretanian	Berber
2. Egyptian/Sudanese	Egyptian Sudanese	Coptic, Nilotic
3. Levantine[1]	Lebanese Syrian Jordanian Palestinian	Local Semitic languages (Aramaic, Phoenician, Canaanite)
4. Arabian Peninsular	Saudi Yemeni Adeni Kuwaiti Gulf (Bahrain, Qatar, the Emirates) Omani	Farsi (in the Gulf states) South Arabian languages
5. Iraqi	Iraqi	Local Semitic languages (Assyrian, Chaldean) Farsi

Speakers of dialects in three of the categories—Egyptian/Sudanese, Levantine, and Arabian Peninsular—have relatively little difficulty understanding each other. The North African and Iraqi dialects (including some Gulf dialects) are relatively difficult for other Arabs to understand.

The most noticeable differences among dialects lie in the vocabulary, although there are grammatical differences too. These differences should be taken into account when choosing a dialect to study. It is almost useless to study a dialect different from the one spoken in the country to which you are going.

Differences tend to be in simple words and phrases, such as greetings, while technical and erudite words are frequently the same. Educated Arabs get around this problem by using classical words, but a foreigner is more likely to experience each dialect as a different language. Examples of differences in dialect are:

Slightly Different

	Egyptian	*Saudi*	*Moroccan*
"paper"	wara'a	waraga	werqa

	Jordanian	*Moroccan*	*Egyptian*
"beautiful"	jameela	jmila	gameela

	Saudi	*Tunisian*	*Lebanese*
"heavy"	tageel	thaqeel	ti'eel

Completely Different

	Lebanese	*Egyptian*	*Iraqi*	*Tunisian*
"How are you?"	keefak?	izzayyak?	shlownak?	shniyya hwalak?

	Moroccan	*Egyptian*	*Jordanian*	*Saudi*
"now"	daba	dilwa'ti	halla'	daheen

	Lebanese	*Kuwaiti*	*Moroccan*	*Egyptian*
"good"	mneeh	zayn	mezyan	kwayyis

Attitudes Toward Dialects

Arabs tend to regard their own dialect as the purest and the closest to Classical Arabic; I have heard this claim vigorously defended from Morocco to Iraq. In fact, where one dialect is closer to the Classical with respect to one feature, another dialect is closer with respect to another. No dialect can be successfully defended as pure except possibly the Najdi dialect spoken in central Arabia, which has been the most isolated from non-Arabic influences.

Arabs view the Bedouin dialects as semi-classical and therefore admirable, although a bit archaic. Most Arabs find the Egyptian dialect to be the most pleasing to listen to because the pronunciation is "light." Eastern Arabs tend to look down on Western Arabic (North African) because of their difficulty in understanding it (which they attribute, wrongly, to Berber usages). Most of the differences between Western and Eastern Arabic stem from changes in pronunciation and word stress.

All Arabs view their local dialect as the best and are quick to advise a foreigner that theirs is the most useful, but usefulness depends entirely on where you are in the Arab World.

Grammatical Structure

The grammatical structure of Arabic is like that of all Semitic languages. Its most striking feature is the way words are formed, which is called the "root and pattern" system. A root is a set of three consonants which carry the *meaning* of the word. The vowels in a word form patterns and, depending on how they are intermixed with the consonants, determine the *part of speech* of a word. The consonants and vowels have different functions in a word, and their combinations yield a rich vocabulary. Here are some examples from Classical Arabic, showing roots and patterns (patterns may contain affixes—additional syllables added at the beginning, in the middle, or at the end of words).

		Meaning
Roots:	k–t–b	"writing"
	r–k–b	"riding"
Patterns:	–a–(a)–a (i)	completed action (past tense)
	–aa–i–	agent (one who does an action)
	ma—a–	place where the action is done
Words:	kataba	"he wrote"
	rakiba	"he rode"
	kaatib	"writer, clerk"
	raakib	"rider"
	maktab	(place for writing) "office, desk"
	markab	(place for riding) "boat"
	markaba	"vehicle"

As you learn vocabulary, you will notice that words which have the same core meaning come in varying patterns but almost all can be reduced to a three-consonant base. For example, other words which share the consonants k–t–b are:

kitaab	"book"
kitaaba	"writing"
maktaba	"library, bookstore"
maktuub	"written, a letter"

Personal names in Arabic usually have a meaning. Here is a group of names from the same three-consonant base, h-m-d, which means "to praise":

Mohamed	Hamdy
Mahmoud	Hammady
Hameed	Hamoud
Hamed	Ahmed

You can see why foreigners sometimes find Arabic names confusing!

Arabic pronunciation makes use of many sounds which do not occur in English, mostly consonants produced far back in the mouth and throat. Some of these consonants show up in the English spelling of words, such as *gh* (Baghdad), *kh* (Khartoum), *q* (Qatar), and *dh* (Riyadh).

In Classical Arabic there are twenty-eight consonants, three long vowels, and three short vowels. In the Arabic dialects some consonants have been dropped or merged with others, and some consonants and vowels have been added—features which distinguish one dialect from another.

Arabic Writing

The Arabic alphabet has twenty-eight letters and is written from right to left. Numerals, however, are written from left to right. The writing is cursive, and most letters connect with the preceding and following letters in the same word. Sometimes two or three sounds are written using the same character; in this case they are differentiated from each other by the arrangement of dots, for example:

b	ب	z	ز
t	ت	s	س
th	ث	sh	ش
r	ر		

Because consonants carry the meaning of words, the Arabic alphabet (like all Semitic alphabets) shows only the consonants and the long vowels (for example, *aa*, which is a different vowel from *a*, and is held twice as long in pronunciation). The short vowels do not appear in the alphabet, but the Arab reader knows what they are and can pronounce the words because these vowels come in predictable patterns. Additional signs (diacritical marks) exist for marking short vowels, doubled consonants and the like, but these are used only in texts for beginners. The signs are, however, always included in the text of the Koran in order to assure correct reading.

The numerals in Arabic are very easy to learn. We refer to our own numbers as "Arabic numerals" because the system of using one symbol for 0 through 9 and adding new place values for "tens," "hundreds," etc., was borrowed from the Arabs to replace the Roman numeral system. Their numerals are used the same way as ours, but they are not alike; note especially their numbers 5 and 6, which look like our 0 and 7:

0	٠	6	٦
1	١	7	٧
2	٢	8	٨
3	٣	9	٩
4	٤	10	١٠
5	٥		

Examples of numbers:

79	790	100	345	1983
٧٩	٧٩٠	١٠٠	٣٤٥	١٩٨٣

There are several styles of handwriting and in each the shapes of the individual letters are slightly different. The difference between North African or Western script, for instance, and Eastern script is especially noticeable.

Decorative calligraphy, of course, is one of the highest artistic expressions of Arab culture. Most letters of the alphabet are full of flowing curves, so an artist can easily form them into elaborate designs. Calligraphy usually depicts Koranic quotations or favorite proverbs, and the patterns are often beautifully balanced and intricate. Calligraphic designs are widely used to decorate mosques, monuments, books, and household items such as brass trays.

Social Greetings

Arabs use many beautiful, elaborate greetings and blessings, and they use them in every type of situation. Most of these expressions are predictable—each situation calls for its own statements and responses.

Situational expressions exist in English, but they are few, such as "How are you?"/"Fine", and "Thank you"/"You're welcome." In Arabic there are at least thirty situations which call for pre-determined expressions. These are burdensome for a student of Arabic to memorize, but it is comforting to know that you can feel secure about what to say in almost every social context.

There are formulas for greetings in the morning and evening, for meeting after a long absence, for meeting the first time, and for welcoming someone who has returned from a trip. There are formulas for acknowledging accomplishments, purchases, marriage, death, for expressing good wishes when someone is drinking a glass of water, engaged in a task, or has just had a haircut! All of these statements have required responses, and they are beautiful in translation and usually religious in content. Some examples are:

English (Statement/Response)	*Arabic Translation (Statement/Response)*
Good morning./Good morning.	Morning of goodness./Morning of light.
Goodbye./Goodbye.	[Go] with safety./May God make you safe.
Happy to see you back./Thanks.	Thanks be to God for your safety./May God make you safe.
(Said when someone is working)	God give you strength./God strengthen you.
(Said when discussing future plans)	May our Lord make it easy.
Good night./Good night.	May you reach morning in goodness./And may you be of the same group.

Social amenities are much used in Arabic. Sometimes an exchange of formalities can last five or ten minutes, particularly among older and more traditional people.

The Arabs have the charming custom of addressing strangers with kinship terms, which connotes respect and good will at the same time. One Western writer was struck by the use of these terms in Yemeni society (they are as widely used elsewhere):

You can tell a people by their words to strangers.
"Brother, how can I help you?"
"Take this taxi, my sisters, I'll find another."
"My mother, it's the best that I can do."
"You're right, uncle."[2]

There are many situations in which verbal statements are required by etiquette. Meeting someone's small child calls for praise, carefully mixed with blessings; the most common are "May God keep him" or "[This is] what God wills." Such statements reassure the parents that there is no envy (you certainly would not add, "I wish I had a child like this!"). Blessings also should be used when seeing something of value, such as a new car ("May you drive it safely") or a new house ("May you live here happily"). When someone purchases something, even a rather small item, the usual word is "Mabrook," which is translated "Congratulations" but literally means "Blessed."

Some of the most-used phrases are given here.

English	Arabic
Hello./Hello.	Marhaba./Marhabtayn.
Good morning./Good morning.	Sabah alkhayr./Sabah annoor.
Peace be upon you./And upon you peace.	Assalamu 'alaykum./Wa 'alaykum assalam.
Goodbye./Goodbye. ([Go] with safety./ May God make you safe.)	Ma'a ssalama./Allah yisallimak.
Thank you./You're welcome.	Shukran./'Afwan.
Congratulations./Thank you. (Blessed./May God bless you.)	Mabrook./Allah yibarik feek.
Welcome./Thanks. (Welcome./ Welcome to you.)	Ahlan wa sahlan./Ahlan beek.

English	*Arabic*
If God wills.	Inshallah (In sha' Allah). Said when speaking of a future event.
What God wills.	Mashallah (Ma sha' Allah). Said when seeing a child or complimenting someone's health.
Thanks be to God.	Alhamdu lillah.
Thanks be to God for your safety.	Hamdillah 'ala ssalama. Said when someone returns from a trip or an illness.

Some Arabic expressions sound much too elaborate to be used comfortably in English. There is no need to use them exactly in translation if you are speaking English, as long as you express good wishes.

Appendix B
The Arab Countries:
Similarities and Differences

Generalizing about the Arabs is a little like generalizing about Europeans—they have many traits in common but regional differences are striking. Arabs have more in common than Europeans, however, because they share the same language and, most importantly, they believe strongly that they are a cultural unit. Arab nationalism has a broad appeal, despite shifting political alliances.

The national, social, and cultural characteristics briefly described below indicate some notable differences between various Arab national groups. The most important single difference which affects foreigners is the distinction between the conservatism of Saudi Arabia and the more liberal, or tolerant, way of life elsewhere.

Morocco

Morocco has been strongly influenced by its proximity to Europe and its colonization by France. Educated Moroccans are bilingual in Arabic and French and, although a campaign of "Moroccanization" has begun, French is still needed for most professional and social advancement. Spanish is widely spoken in northern Morocco.

Most Moroccans are descended from native Berber stock; a few can also trace Arabian origins. The royal family traces its descent from the Prophet Mohamed. There are also many Moroccans of Black African origin, especially in the southern part of the country. About 33 to 40% of the population are Berbers who speak their own language and mainly inhabit the interior highlands.

There are three distinct social classes in Morocco: the royal family and a small educated elite, a middle class comprised of merchants and professionals, and a lower class which includes more than half of the people. The population growth rate is among the highest in the world. Thousands of Moroccan men work outside the country, mainly in France, because of widespread unemployment at home.

Tribalism is important in Morocco, particularly in the rural areas, and traditional farming is the occupation of about half of the population.[1] The cities are growing rapidly, with a trend toward urbanization which began early in this century. This has resulted in many poor and underemployed urban residents, and slums are growing. The food supply is unevenly distributed, and at least 20% of the people are poorly nourished.[2] There is a serious housing shortage in urban areas and health care is not yet adequate.

Education has increased greatly since Morocco's independence in 1956, but in 1978, 85% of the people were still illiterate.[3] Both Arabic and French are taught in the schools. Education is now available to girls. Although few Moroccan women are active in the work force other than in domestic service, educated women are increasing their role in the professions, especially in the urban areas. Older and conservative Moroccan women veil in public, but "modernized" women do not, nor do they wear the long cloak worn by traditional women.

Almost all Moroccans are Moslems, although other religions have always been tolerated. There are still 20,000 Jews and many Christians of European origin in the country. The practice of Islam is often mixed with local folk practices, such as the veneration of holy men or saints' tombs and artifacts. Religious brotherhoods are also common.

The Moroccan economy is largely dependent upon agriculture, tourism, and phosphate mining; Morocco is the world's largest exporter of phosphates.

Moroccans are friendly and hospitable and usually very interested in becoming acquainted with foreigners. The elite are quite at ease with Westerners due to their exposure to French and European culture.

Algeria

Algeria is a revolutionary socialist state where "Arabization" is strongly emphasized, partly as a reaction to the Algerians' experience with French colonization and the long, traumatic war for independence which was achieved in 1962. French is widely spoken, and only the younger Algerians who are now in school are truly comfortable with literary Arabic. Arabic is the official language of the country, but it has not replaced French for professional purposes; both languages are taught in the schools.

Arab nationalism is strong in Algeria. There is a concerted effort to promote it through government political campaigns, the news media, and the school curriculum. Most Algerians are of Berber ethnic origin. Arabic is the native language of 80% of the people; the others speak Berber or are bilingual. There are also 1,000 native Jews in Algeria.

Algeria's social classes consist of a small professional and technocratic elite, a growing middle class, and a large number of poor people. The long war resulted in the displacement of many people who lost ties with ancestral land and social groups, and the psychological consequences will be felt for another generation.

About half of Algeria's people work in agriculture. Two-thirds of the country is part of the Sahara Desert, but there is excellent agricultural land in the temperate northern coastal region. Several thousand Algerian men work outside the country, mainly in France, because local salaries are low and prices are very high. Unemployment is a serious problem; people continue to move from the sparsely-populated south to the crowded northern cities.

Despite the government's high priority on health and education programs, they have not greatly benefited most of the people. Living conditions and diet are poor for the lower classes, and the population growth rate is too high to be adequately accommodated.

A growing number of educated Algerians are entering professional and technical fields. There were few well-trained Algerians at the time of independence, and it has taken time to recover from the loss of the French managerial class. Women in Algeria are not as active in the work force as they are in neighboring countries. Family and social traditions are very conservative, and more women veil in Algeria than in any other North African country.

Over 99% of the Algerians are Moslem, and Islam is practiced in conjunction with local folk practices.

Algeria is the world's largest producer of liquified natural gas, and it also has income from oil, mining, and agriculture. The government is trying to diversify and industrialize the economy.

Algerians are polite and accommodating, but reserved. They are generally directed inward toward their own society, although many younger people are becoming interested in befriending foreigners.

Tunisia

Tunisia is a small but diverse country which became independent from France in 1956. It has been governed by one political party since independence, and the government is quite liberal. Tunisia has always had contact with foreigners and, as a result, its society is cosmopolitan, at least in the cities. The Tunisian people have been described as one-third modern, one-third transitional, and one third traditional.[4]

The Tunisians are descended from Berber and Arab stock but all speak Arabic, which is the official language. Educated people are bilingual in Arabic and French and many semi-educated people also speak French. Arabic and French are both taught in the schools; a campaign of "Arabization" has begun.

The Tunisian government encourages private enterprise, with the result that a large number of Tunisians are in the prosperous upper and middle classes—about 40% in 1976.[5] The majority of the people, however, are quite poor, and salaries are low. Many of the poor spend up to 75% of their income on food.[6]

About half of the Tunisian people work in agriculture, and the northern two thirds of the country is good for farming and grazing. The government has established agricultural cooperatives, and production has been rising. There is a trend for people to move to the cities where the poor often live in crowded conditions.

The Tunisian government spends a large proportion of its money on education, which is widely available. A growing social problem is the number of unemployed educated young people. Many Tunisian men work outside the country, mainly in France and Libya.

Tunisia has been at the forefront of the Arab nations in its efforts to liberalize traditional social values. Tunisian women are rapidly becoming more active in the work force and many are well educated; they work, for example, in education, social services, health care, and office administration. While most women wear Western clothing, older or traditional women wear a loose outer cloak which they use to partially cover their face when in public.

Ninety-eight percent of the Tunisians are Moslem; there are also about 9,000 native Jews, and some Christians of

European origin. The practice of Islam is intermixed with a number of local folk beliefs.

The Tunisian economy depends on agricultural exports, tourism, and the production of some oil and natural gas. The government is encouraging diversification and light industry.

Tunisians are industrious and resourceful, and many are well-traveled. They are friendly and hospitable to their friends and to visitors to their country.

Libya

Libya is the only North African nation which was colonized by Italy. Full rule was restored to the monarchy in 1949; it was overthrown in 1969 and since then, Libya has been governed by a leftist military regime. The new regime introduced radical socialist and economic development programs and the society has undergone rapid change. There is a strong campaign to educate and politicize the people.

Until recently, most Libyans outside the cities were farmers or tribal semi-nomads who were largely uneducated and lived at a simple level. The country has poor soil, poor natural resources, and little water. The discovery of oil, and its effect on the economy, began in 1961; by 1969, the country's revenues were twenty times greater than in 1962.[7] Libya is a welfare state, and a good share of its oil income is being enjoyed by the lower classes, who have experienced a dramatic rise in their standard of living. Health and nutrition programs, transportation, and communications are improving steadily.

The Libyans are a homogeneous ethnic group, of mixed Berber and Arab descent, and all speak Arabic. Tribalism is an important source of identity, particularly among the rural people. There are no "recognized" social classes now, due to the government's policy of strict egalitarianism and rule "by the people." In reality, rule is authoritarian, and only a few of the people are in the elite upper class.

Libya is sparsely populated; only 10% of the land is suitable for agriculture, 90% is desert. Nevertheless, in the late 70's, 80% of the people were engaged in farming.[8] There is a trend toward moving from the rural areas to the cities.

Libya's economic viability is almost entirely dependent on oil. Because it badly needs trained and skilled workers, there are large numbers of foreigners working there.

Universal education has been available only since the 1970's, and now about 20% of the people are literate. Libya supports about 10,000 university students abroad, most of them in the United States.

Libyan society is conservative, and Islamic law is generally followed, although some of the legal traditions have been discarded.[9] Libyan women are becoming moderately educated, but they rarely work outside the home and usually marry young. The role of women is much discussed and in the last decade there has been some encouragement for women to work. Free intermingling between men and women is culturally unacceptable, however, so they work in fields such as teaching, nursing, clerical services, and some factory jobs.[10]

The Libyans are Moslem, and the government promotes an "Islamic revival" mixed with a revolutionary message in order to control social changes. Arab nationalism and pan-Arab unity are extolled and the Western way of life is denigrated. As a result of this emphasis, Libyans are not particularly outgoing toward foreigners, and many realize that such associations could lead to a police investigation.

Egypt

Egypt has a long tradition of civilization and unification and has a homogeneous society which is distinctive—many Egyptian attitudes, traits and practices are uniquely their own. The government has been socialist since 1952 and has been stable. Egyptians all speak Arabic, except for some Nubians in the far south. English is the most common second language, and French is also spoken by many.

Egypt has the largest population of any Arab nation, and its density is among the highest in the world, 1260 per square kilometer in 1983.[11] The population of the country doubled between 1947 and the early 1980's, with a subsequent strain on housing, schools, and public services, especially in the cities.

Only a small percentage of the Egyptians are in the elite upper class which dominates the country socially and politically. The middle class is expanding rapidly. About 60% of the people are peasant farmers or villagers.[12]

Intensive agriculture is central to the Egyptian economy, but only 5% of the land is arable, because the fertile Nile Valley is bounded by desert on both sides. Industrial manufacturing has been promoted by the government, with products such as iron and steel, aluminum, and fertilizer. The main sources of the country's income are oil, cotton and other agricultural products, and tourism.

The Egyptian people are hard-working and generally well-nourished, but poor. Health is improving due to government programs instituted in the 1960's.

There is a long tradition of education for the upper and middle classes, and Egypt has an abundance of professional people. About 15% of the total work force were employed abroad in the mid-1970's;[13] they were trained people such as teachers, doctors, and accountants, as well as laborers. Most Egyptians working abroad are in the Arabian peninsula and Libya. Salaries in Egypt are low, and local prices are rising. Because of the large number of educated people, upward mobility is slow. Since the 1960's, free education has been available to all of the country's children.

Egyptian women have enjoyed considerable personal freedom in pursuing their interests and have been integrated into the work force at all levels for a generation. Between 1960 and

1976 the number of women in universities increased sixfold.[14] Egyptian women discarded the veil 50 years ago, but many wear very conservative dress.

About 93% of the Egyptians are Moslems, and the rest are native Christians, mostly Copts. Religious tolerance has been practiced despite the government's proclamation of Islam as the official religion. Religiosity is on the rise, however, and the society, which was among the most liberal in the Arab World, is becoming more conservative.

Egypt is vibrant with cultural energy, and it is the leader of the Arab nations in such fields as filmmaking and journalism. It has long been an important political and cultural influence in the Arab World. Once a strong promoter of Arab nationalism, the government has now mellowed somewhat and turned much of its attention inward.

The Egyptian people are lively, friendly, good-humored and emotional. They are very outgoing toward foreigners.

Sudan

Sudan (also called The Sudan) is the largest country in Africa. There is considerable African influence on its social structure and ethnic composition. It is tribal and diverse, and Arabic is spoken by only 51% of the population.[15] There are more than 100 native languages spoken, and in many areas the first two years of school are taught in the local language.

Sudanese in the north are Arabized and Moslem and often bilingual in Arabic and their regional language. Arabic is the official language, and it is needed for social advancement. About 10% of the southerners are Christian, and the rest follow regional pagan practices. The government has decreed Islam as the official religion and recently imposed Islamic law throughout the country.

The Sudanese government is socialist, and it is attempting to bring about a more nationalist and unifying sentiment in the country. A civil war between the Arab north and the African south was fought from 1955 to 1972, and was settled by the government's commitment to giving southerners more substantial participation in society and politics. Some tension is still evident, and the various groups of people do not yet share common values or economic ties. Many southern tribes live autonomously, barely influenced by the government. Tribalism is dominant throughout the society, and many men are marked with identifying facial scars, as is common throughout sub-Sahara Africa.

Population density is low in Sudan; the northern cities are growing, but rural areas are thinly settled. About 80% of the Sudanese people are villagers and small farmers or herders. The government has only recently begun planning irrigation and land reclamation programs to develop the immense agricultural potential of much of the country.

Education and health programs have been established, but they have not yet reached a large part of the population, particularly in the south. The health of the people is often poor due to tropical conditions, inadequate diet, and great distances between settlements. In the north, education has been available for the upper and middle classes for 50 years, and there are many well-educated professionals in the country. Because of low salaries at home, many people are working abroad, both as professionals and as laborers, mainly in the Arabian peninsula. This has caused a shortage of trained manpower in the country.

Few urban Sudanese women work outside the home, although women are now being educated. Some women are working in social work and teaching.

Sudan has one of the poorest and least developed economies in the world,[16] and the government is presently imposing an austerity program to improve its balance of payments. It lacks money for some much-needed projects, such as roads and communications. Sudan's main sources of income are agricultural products and, increasingly, oil.

The Sudanese are known for being friendly, sincere, generous, and scrupulously honest, and they are proud of this reputation. They are conservative and religious.

Lebanon

Lebanon is a small country with a diverse geography and a long history of commercial and maritime importance. The people are mainly descended from the same Semitic stock, but religious diversity and social class have divided them into many self-contained groups and this has been a barrier to social integration. All Lebanese feel an intense loyalty to their own clan or religious group. This, combined with the fact that Christians have traditionally had more wealth and power than the more numerous Moslems, finally led to tensions which resulted in the civil war. A third influential denomination is the Druze religion, which originated in Lebanon in the 17th century, and is derived from Islam.

The religious diversity of Lebanon is extreme. The population is about 60% Moslem and 40% Christian. About 28% of the Lebanese are Christians of the native Maronite rite, and there are at least twelve other Christian denominations. About 26% of the people are Sunni (or orthodox) Moslems, and 27% are Shiite Moslems.[17]

The Lebanese speak Arabic, and educated people also speak French or English, or both. There are some minority groups, such as Armenians and Kurds, who speak their own languages.

Prior to the beginning of the civil war in 1975, the Lebanese government was pro-Western and pro-capitalist, and the country was a leader in service industries such as banking, commerce, and tourism. The Lebanese had the highest standard of living in the Arab World, and the most cosmopolitan, sophisticated way of life, at least in Beirut. After Cairo, Beirut was the second largest center for the diffusion of Arab culture. By contrast, however, the rural Lebanese have always been very conservative and traditional.

Lebanese have migrated abroad in great numbers since the late 19th century, and contact with these emigrants all over the world has influenced the society in the home country. Many Lebanese work in other Arab countries, mainly as managers and professionals. The Lebanese are known for their intelligence, excellent commercial ability, and resourcefulness.

There are clear social classes in Lebanon. In 1983, the wealthy upper class comprised about 18% of the people, about 30% were in the middle class, and about half of the people were in the lower class.[18] People in the lower class are quite poor, and many of them live in villages or work as farmers. Agricultural production is limited by poor natural resources, and imports far exceed exports.

The Lebanese are generally well-educated, particularly those who live in or near urban areas. In the late 19th century, French and American missionaries established schools which trained many of the future leaders and influenced the society toward a westernized way of thought. Even today, large numbers of Lebanese are educated in denominational private schools, and attendance at a good school affects a person's future opportunities. Free public education has long been available in Lebanon, and its literacy rate is about 90%, the highest in the Middle East. Health care and social services are of a high standard.

Many urban Lebanese women, especially Christians, are highly educated and active in the professions, commerce, and social activities. Women in rural areas are restricted by the traditional values which predominate.

The Lebanese people are very interested in politics and their position in the world. Some, mainly Christians, believe that Lebanon should be more western than Arab and orient its identity toward Europe; others, mainly Moslems, identify with pan-Arab sentiments and would like to de-emphasize westernization. Urban Christians are generally liberal in their way of life, while urban Moslems and rural people of all religions are more conservative.

Syria

Syria has a long history of civilization which often attained a very high level, but its history is also one of frequent invasions and conquests, mainly due to its strategic location. Its population is fairly diverse, and to some extent Syrian society lacks cohesiveness.

About 90% of the people are Moslems, of whom 70% are Sunni, and the rest belong to other Islamic sects. The Alawites, a Shiite sect, are the largest ethno-religious minority group with 12% of the population, and they presently control the government. Some other minority groups include Christians, 10%; Druze, 3%; Kurds, 10%; and smaller numbers of Armenians, Jews, and Assyrians.[19] The ethnic and religious groups tend to concentrate in certain geographic areas.

Arabic is the official language, spoken by nearly all Syrians. Many speak French as a second language, and knowledge of English is growing. Minorities speak languages such as Kurdish, Turkish, Armenian, Syriac, and Aramaic.

Syria has a revolutionary socialist government which is authoritarian, strongly nationalistic, strongly anti-Israel, and cautious in its relations with the West. Various governments underwent many coups in the first years of independence since 1946, but the present government has remained in power since 1970. Its stability has made possible recent government-promoted social changes.

Syria is one of the most densely populated Arab countries because only about half of its land is habitable. Its population growth rate is very high. It has several major cities, and in the rural areas, intensive farming has made agricultural produce an important factor in the economy. Other sources of revenue include oil, phosphates, and textiles.

Syrians in the upper and middle class comprise about 25% of the people.[20] They are well educated and have a high standard of living. Syria has many well-trained professionals in various fields. Public education has reached everyone since the 1960's. Government health centers are established in cities and rural areas. Land reform and the establishment of agricultural cooperatives have led to some improvements in the lives of small farmers who comprise about half of the population; agriculture boomed in the 1970's. The standard of living for urban workers has also improved.

Most Syrians identify strongly with Arab nationalistic aspirations and their Moslem heritage. They are generally quite conservative. Syrian women of the upper class have been well-educated for a generation, and are moderately active in the work force, especially as teachers and social or health care workers. Education for girls has resulted in an increasing number of women at work. Few women wear a veil in tribes or villages; it is often worn by older or conservative women in the towns and cities.

Syrians are bright, friendly, talkative, and very hospitable to friends and guests. They are interested in world events and enjoy discussions about any range of subjects. Some of them have been wary of too much contact with Westerners, however, because government policy toward the West is variable.

Jordan

Jordan was created as a nation under British mandate only at the end of the First World War, and became independent in 1946. There has not been enough time to form a homogeneous, truly "Jordanian" society, although a Jordanian identity has begun to develop among the elite and in the cities. Jordan's West Bank, which is under occupation, was formerly a part of Palestine, and the East Bank area was originally tied by tribal affiliations with northwest Saudi Arabia. Thus, Jordanian citizens are of both Palestinian and Bedouin origin, and at least until the 1970's, the royal family depended on its Bedouin kinsmen for support and viability.[21] Tribalization is rapidly giving way as more people settle in or near cities. The government sponsors a sedentarization program.

Jordan's monarchist government is moderate and pro-Western, and the people are, on the whole, prosperous. There are clear social classes—a small upper class, a growing middle class, and the large lower class, mainly comprised of farmers, villagers, and refugees. In general, the standard of living in Jordan is high.

Jordanians speak Arabic, and educated people speak English as a second language.

Ninety-three percent of the Jordanians are Sunni Moslems, and about 5% are Christians. Religious tolerance is very good on both sides and is not a divisive factor in the society. Jordan is at a geographic crossroad between neighboring countries, and the people have traditionally been tolerant and hospitable, retaining Bedouin values.

Agriculture is a major factor in the economy of the West Bank, but there is little fertile land in the eastern area and only about 20% of the people are farmers. There are still a few nomadic herders in the east but most are settling in villages. Jordanians also work in industry and service trades, and about half are employed by the government and the armed forces.[22] The economy of the country is based on tourism, mining, industry, trade, and agriculture.

Jordanians are enjoying a constantly improving quality of life, due to well-established health and education programs. About 70% of the people are literate.

Many Jordanians are in professional and technical fields, and many work outside the country, mostly in the Arabian peninsula. There are large numbers of well-trained professionals in Jordan.

Jordanian social values are quite conservative, although

there is a trend toward becoming more "modern" in the cosmopolitan city of Amman. The influx of Palestinians into the country contributed to the impetus to modernize. Many Jordanian women are well-educated, and working in a wide variety of fields, including teaching, nursing, and clerical work. They do not wear a veil.

The Jordanians are very personable, warm, and welcoming. They enjoy friendships with foreigners.

Iraq

Iraq, like Syria, has a long tradition of civilization and a proud history, but its achievements were set back time after time by invasions and conquests. Unlike heavily populated Egypt, Iraq is underpopulated—although its land is as fertile and its history as old—mainly as a result of repeated violence and devastation. The location and geography of Iraq have made it a strategic battlefield area.

About 71% of the Iraqis are Arabs, and 18% are Kurds who speak their own language. There are also minority ethnic groups, the main ones being Turkomans, Assyrians, Armenians, and some Iranian-origin peoples. Arabic is the official language, spoken by the majority of the people. English is widely spoken by educated people.

Iraq has been strongly influenced by its Islamic heritage because several sites sacred to Shiite Moslems are located there and are the object of religious pilgrimages. Ninety-five percent of the Iraqis are Moslems, of whom 52% are Shiite.[23] Four percent of the people are Christians. Iraqis are devout and their social values are conservative.

The Iraqi government is revolutionary socialist and was established after the monarchy was overthrown in 1958. There have been four coups since then; the present government has been in power since 1968. It is authoritarian and, until recently, was the main source of opposition to Western interests in the Arabian Gulf area. A small elite group has most of the social and political influence.

Education for the upper class goes back 40 years, and Iraq has many well-trained professional people. Public education became available universally in the 1960's and 70's.

The government has established development projects to increase agriculture and industry. In 1973, only 18% of the land was cultivated[24] and efforts are underway to reclaim much more. There are also public health programs which reach most of the population. All such activities, however, were subordinated to the war effort; the war with Iran has been a great drain on resources.

Iraq's major source of income is its oil, but it also has income from agriculture and animal products, and textiles. Many foreigners, especially Egyptians, are imported for agricultural work.

Iraqi women are becoming better educated but they are still a small percentage of the people in the labor force. Many upper-class women are well educated; most work in the fields of teaching, clerical work, and health care.

The Iraqis are very hard-working and patriotic. They are rather reserved but very polite to foreigners and willing to be helpful.

Saudi Arabia

Saudi Arabia is a new nation. It was a loosely-governed area inhabited by numerous Bedouin tribes, with a few urban centers of commerce on or near the western coast, until it was united in 1935 by King Abdel-Aziz ibn Saud. His descendants still rule. Since unification, Saudi Arabia has developed into a viable nation and society, and the Saudi people have a national identity.

Saudis are Sunni Moslems except for a few thousand Shiites on the eastern coast. Most Saudis still have a tribal and regional affiliation, although tribalism as a socio-political unit is losing much of its meaning as modern society develops.[25] All Saudis speak Arabic; Saudi Arabia is where the Arabic language originated.

The two most important factors which influence Saudi society are the historical fact that their homeland was the birthplace of Islam, and the discovery of oil which led to sudden wealth. Oil was first produced in 1938, but the real effects of wealth were felt throughout the society beginning in the 1960's. Religiosity, conservatism, wealth, foreign workers . . . all of these factors are present at once in Saudi Arabia, and their mixture results in ever-changing attitudes, policies, social plans, and reactions. The final shape of Saudi society is still unclear.

Saudis engage in a great deal of public soul-searching, evaluation, and comparison of their and others' way of life. They adhere to the austere Wahhabi sect of Islam. They uphold traditional values such as observing religious practices strictly, retaining filial piety and family control, and restricting the role of women. These now seem threatened, so the authorities are reacting strongly. The "rules" are changing, and for foreigners they are becoming more restrictive in many ways—they affect, for example, manner of dress, the absolute prohibition of alcohol, socializing between men and women, control of the media, and the practice of religions other than Islam. In this respect, Saudi Arabian society is by far the most authoritarian in the Arab World; even other Arabs need time to adjust. Penalties for non-compliance are severe.

In a nation of only 7 million people, there are 1 to 1½ million foreign workers.[26] They must be tolerated as long as they are needed, but Saudis are trying hard to place their own people in management and professional positions (there is a traditional aversion to manual work).[27] Upward mobility is rapid for young university graduates. There is a new trend to recruit Oriental workers in preference to Westerners because they stay to themselves and constitute less of a cultural influence and threat.[28]

Health and education programs got underway in the 1960's, with far-reaching results. Public health facilities, specialized medical care, adult education, and schooling through the university level are available free of charge to all citizens. Saudi Arabian society will undoubtedly change as much in the next twenty years as it has in the past twenty.

The social classes of Saudi Arabia are royalty, followed by the growing class of educated elite, growing middle class, and the uneducated lower class. The latter may be poor, but just as often they are simply isolated from services and living in their traditional manner.

Saudi women are entering the work force in ever larger numbers, but are restricted to working in all-female environments. They are anxious to become more active in society and to contribute what they can to developing their country. They are fully veiled in public, and cannot travel alone or drive cars.

The Saudis are reserved and are not quick to accept foreigners into their personal lives. A non-relative may, in fact, never meet the women in a Saudi's family. Once a friendship is established, however, the Saudis are generous and hospitable in the time-honored Arab way.

North and South Yemen

Historical Yemen is now divided into two states—North Yemen has a socialist government, while South Yemen (formerly Aden) has a Marxist government. This area was long isolated from outside contact and influences, and is still one of the most colorful and traditional areas in the Arab World.

The line separating the country was drawn in 1904 by Ottoman and British representatives who controlled North and South Yemen respectively. Power in North Yemen was gradually won by the former ruling family during the early years of the twentieth century. The British left the south in 1967, at which time a Marxist government was established which resulted in the exodus of one fourth of the population.[29] There has been some talk of unification, but this is hampered by deep disparities in the two countries' political and social structures. A civil war was waged from 1962 to 1969, and in 1972, tensions again escalated to a full-scale war which ultimately ended through mediation by the Arab League.

In both Yemeni states, society is stratified, and people belong at birth to one of several tribes and classes that resemble in their rigidity the castes of India.[30] Marriage between social groups is difficult; in general, women cannot marry into inferior groups.

Yemenis are all Moslem Arabs. In the north, the most distinctive division is between the Sunni Moslems and the Zaidi sect which dates to the 13th century; each group has well-defined geographic boundaries. In the south, the people are almost all Sunni, and there has been much intermarriage with African and Indian peoples.

Yemenis speak Arabic in the form of some unique dialects in remote areas. Educated Yemenis speak English as a second language.

The society in North Yemen has changed little since modernization programs were introduced beginning in the late 60's; indeed, much of the country is still emerging from primitivism. Many people live in remote villages. High mountains and a temperate climate have made possible intensive agriculture, much of it on terraced land. Coffee and cotton are also a big source of revenue. Traditional skills include construction and stone masonry, carpentry, and metal work. Thousands of Yemenis are employed in these trades in Saudi Arabia, and their remittances are an important part of the economy. Most Yemeni men chew a mildly euphoria-producing leaf called "qat," beginning in early afternoon every day; as a result, productivity is lessened and life moves at a leisurely pace.

South Yemen has a semi-arid climate, and the people were traditionally herders and farmers, as well as merchants in the coastal cities. South Yemen's geographical location has been good for commerce with the Indian Ocean area and for fishing. The government has now nationalized businesses, confiscated large land and residential holdings, and collectivized trades. A large share of the income comes from the procurement and distribution of petroleum products.

Health programs are growing in the north, but there is still a high infant mortality rate, poor sanitation, and a lack of awareness of general health practices. Most children are now in school, which will soon affect the present low literacy rate.

In the south, health care is hampered by a severe shortage of qualified people, and its availability is limited to the Aden area. The government has launched a crash education program, which includes adults. Emphasis is on science, engineering, and technology.

Women in North Yemen are fully veiled in public and almost all are uneducated and do not work outside the home. In South Yemen, women have been granted equal status by law, and they are being recruited into the labor force, where they work in fields such as accounting and mechanics or in factories. Women are more integrated into society in South Yemen than in any other Arabian peninsular country.[31]

Yemenis are admired because they are so industrious, skilled, and quick to learn. They are friendly and curious about the outside world, and very accommodating to foreigners.

Kuwait

Kuwait is a small but influential country, mostly because of its vast oil wealth and its subsequent economic and political influence among the Arab states. It became independent of British protectorate status in 1961, and is ruled by an emir. Rule is entirely in the hands of the royal family; a popularly-elected assembly was tried briefly but dissolved.

In many ways, Kuwaiti society resembles Saudi society, in

that it is tribal, religious, and conservative, and the two countries have long had close ties. Kuwaitis are Arab Moslems; over 90% are Sunni, and the rest are Shiites. Their sect of Islam is not as austere as that in Saudi Arabia.

The dominant fact of life in Kuwait is the government's enormous wealth. Per capita income is the highest in the world.[32] Production of oil was begun in 1946 and Kuwait experienced a great influx of people. Within 15 years after oil revenue began, poverty was virtually abolished,[33] and Kuwait is now a welfare state. Kuwait has the reputation of being the shrewdest and most sophisticated of the big Arab overseas investors.[34]

There are strong class distinctions and class consciousness in Kuwait, and wealth is becoming ever more widespread. Kuwait began its development process about 20 years before Saudi Arabia, and as a result, it is much more "settled." Being so small, and having a homogeneous (often interrelated) population, there are fewer interest groups to consider and it is easier to reach all of the people.

Progress in health, education, and economic development has completely changed the way of life in the last 30 years. The process of social change is finally leveling off now that most goals have been achieved. The opportunity for upward mobility and high-responsibility employment is excellent for young people.

More than half of the people in Kuwait are immigrants; Palestinians constitute over one third of the residents. There are so many foreign workers in the country that they constitute about 80% of the work force.[35] Kuwait is more tolerant of foreigners and their practices than is Saudi Arabia, although recently it has imposed some new restrictions which may herald a trend.

Kuwaiti women are veiled in public, and while many are well-educated, they do not usually work. Some women are teachers or work in women's organizations; a few own their own businesses. Unlike Saudi Arabia, Kuwait does not have a prohibition against women working in the same environment as men.[36]

Kuwaitis tend to prefer their private and family social circles. They are helpful to foreigners, but not quick to establish strong personal friendships.

The Arabian Gulf States

The Arabian Gulf states considered together here include Bahrain, Qatar, the United Arab Emirates, and Oman. They are situated on the eastern coast of the Arabian peninsula and were, until 1971, under British administration as the Trucial States.

This area has the world's largest oil and natural gas deposits (shared with Iraq, Kuwait, Saudi Arabia, and Iran), so the Gulf states are all newly prosperous and changing rapidly. Their territories are quite small and natural resources are few except for fishing. All other sources of revenue are dwarfed by revenue from the oil sector. They have conservative, traditional societies.

Bahrain is the most modernized state in the Gulf, and it was the first Gulf state to produce oil. Its oil revenues are small compared to the neighboring states, and they are declining. The government has diversified into drydock ship services, aluminum production, and light engineering. Bahrain is an important banking center and also has excellent tourist facilities. It is ruled by an emir.

Bahrainis are Arab Moslems, and the population is about evenly split between Sunnis and Shiites; this division is the most serious threat to continued stability. About half of the people live in the capital city of Manama. Arabic is the official language, and English is widely used as a second language.

Bahrain's small size and population contributed to its rapid modernization. Education and health programs are universally available, and only 35% of the workers in Bahrain are foreign. In 1974–75 a survey showed that women were active

in 5 to 10% of the occupations which require a formal education and 82% of the Bahraini women with college degrees
were working.[37]

Qatar is a peninsula which is rich in both oil and natural gas
and offers great employment and commercial opportunities.
After oil entered the economy in 1949, Qatar's population
almost doubled; about 80% of the work force are foreigners.

Until 30 years ago, the Qatari people were engaged in
fishing, pearling, and trading, and many lived in dire poverty. Now their lives are being transformed by education and
health programs, and state subsidies. Full literacy will be
attained by the next generation. In 1975, 44% of the Qataris
were under the age of 15.[38]

Qatar is ruled by an emir, and the society is very conservative; it is the only other country which follows the same
puritanical Wahhabi sect of Islam as Saudi Arabia. The country is so small that the emir runs it like a family business, and
he rules in conjunction with an advisory council. All of the
Qataris are Arab Moslems. They speak Arabic, and English is
used as the second language.

Qatar's social organization is tribal, and family orientation
is strong. Qatar's young men are beginning to assume professional and managerial positions. One observer characterized
young Qataris in a way that applies equally well to the youth
of any of the newly-rich states—since they are basically free
of anxiety regarding money or employment, they are looking
for a job with status, prestige, and authority within the shortest possible time, not always a realistic goal.[39]

Qatari women are now being educated, but they are not
yet very active in the work force. Over 80% of the women are
married between the ages of 15 and 20.[40]

The United Arab Emirates is a federation of small territories created in 1971 by uniting seven of the trucial states. Abu
Dhabi is the largest and the capital; Dubai is the main port and
commercial center. The union has worked out well on the
whole; rulers of the smaller areas realize that they have at-

tained more influence and economic benefit through alliance with larger neighbors. The people are Arab Moslems, and almost all are Sunni.

Abu Dahbi began oil production in 1962, Dubai in 1969, and Sharjah in 1973.[41] The other four emirates have no oil, and are experiencing relatively little economic growth or social change, compared with Abu Dhabi and Dubai. Abu Dhabi's oil income accounts for 80% of the UAE's earnings; per capita income is the second-highest in the Gulf area. About 75% of the residents in the UAE are foreign workers.

Ambitious programs have been established in education, health, and agricultural production since the present ruler took power in 1966, and these are just beginning to affect the general population. Tribalism is gradually breaking down as wage-earning and modernization increase, but the society is still very traditional, with conservative social values in place. Women are veiled and participate little in public life.

Oman has a rich maritime history, and it is geographically strategic. It is ruled by a sultan, and only since oil production began in 1967 have enthusiastic modernization programs been started. British domination ceased officially in 1971, but remained a powerful force until 1975.

About seven eighths of the population of Oman are Arabs, and others are of Baluchi, Indian, or black African origin. Almost all of the people speak Arabic. Most Omanis are Moslems of the moderate Ibadi sect, and because this is different from people in the surrounding countries, it has contributed to an isolationist tendency. The second-largest group are Sunni, followed by the Shiites, who usually live in their own communities. The principal non-Moslem minority group are Indian Hindus, who have been resident in Oman for several centuries.

Tribalism is still the main source of identity for the Omani people, although tribal power has declined since the beginning of the oil economy. The social, economic, and political organization of Oman derived to a large extent from the importance of oasis agriculture, although now the remote interior settlements have more contact with the rest of the country. There is a physical and psychological dichotomy between the coast and the interior. The coastal people are an ethnocultural mixture, and it is this area which has provided a stable base for the ruling family. About 95% of Oman's people live outside of the cities.[42]

The majority of the people still work in agriculture, and Oman has a large area of potentially arable land. It lacks manpower, however, and there is a shortage of water. Omani citizens work at all levels, including manual labor; they are not wealthy enough to avoid that. There are many foreign workers; it is estimated that by the mid-80's, Oman will have over 1½ million foreign residents from the Indian subcontinent and the Far East alone, or about 55% of the foreign work force.[43]

Omani women are more visible than in the rest of the Arabian peninsula, but they are still restricted by traditional social practice. The government encourages women's education, and many continue their education even after marriage, which commonly occurs at age 18 or younger. Women who work have jobs in a female environment such as teaching; women who are descendants of families which have returned from Africa are generally freer and some of them are professionals in a variety of fields.

Notes

Introduction

1. Nyrop, Richard, ed., *Saudi Arabia, A Country Study*, p. 100.
2. Nyrop, Richard, ed., *Jordan, A Country Study*, p. 98.
3. Nyrop, Richard, ed., *Iraq, A Country Study*, p. 108.
4. *The Middle East and North Africa 1979-80*, p. 695.
5. Khouja, M.W. and Sadler, P.G., *The Economy of Kuwait—Development and Role in International Finance*, p. 33.
6. *Kingdom of Saudi Arabia Statistical Yearbook*, pp. 80-87.
7. *The Middle East and North Africa 1979-80*, p. 696.
8. *Ibid.*, p. 319 and p. 328.
9. Omran, Abdel-Rahim, *Population in the Arab World*, pp. 74-75.
10. Khouja and Sadler, *The Economy of Kuwait*, p. 33.
11. Parssinen, Catherine, "The Changing Role of Women," in *King Faisal and the Modernisation of Saudi Arabia*, p. 160.
12. "$1.1 Billion Being Spent on Girls' Schools," *Arab News*, September 13, 1983.
13. Nyrop, ed., *Jordan, A Country Study*, p. 102.
14. "Oman: An Introduction," *Aramco World*, May/June, 1983, p. 2.
15. Al-Farsy, Fouad, *Saudi Arabia—A Case Study in Development*, p. 147.
16. Omran, *Population in the Arab World*, p. 113.
17. *Ibid.*, p. 53.
18. *Ibid.*, pp. 100-101.

19. *Ibid.*, p. 101.

20. Nyrop, ed., *Jordan, A Country Study,* pp. 66-67.

21. Omran, *Population in the Arab World,* pp. 32-35.

22. Algosaibi, Ghazi A., "Arabs and Western Civilization," in *Arabian Essays,* pp. 16-17.

23. Hottinger, Arnold, "The Depth of Arab Radicalism," pp. 498-99.

24. Laroui, Abdallah, *Crisis of the Arab Intellectual,* p. 165.

25. Husain, S.S. and Ashraf, S.A., eds., *Crisis in Muslim Education,* p. 2.

26. *Ibid.*, p. 13.

27. *Ibid.*, pp. 37-38

28. *Ibid.*, p. 72.

29. Qutb, Muhammad, "The Role of Religion in Education," in *Aims and Objectives of Islamic Education,* pp. 56-60.

30. Thomas and Deakin, *The Arab Experience,* p. 23

31. Melikian, Levon H., "The Modal Personality of Saudi College Students: A Study in National Character," in *Psychological Dimensions of Near Eastern Studies,* p. 172.

32. El-Sadat, Anwar, *In Search of Identity,* p. 6.

33. Willis, David K., "The Impact of Islam," *The Christian Science Monitor,* p. 11.

34. Sardar, Ziauddin, *Science, Technology, and Development in the Muslim World,* pp. 55-56.

35. El Guindi, Fadwa," Is There an Islamic Alternative? The Case of Egypt's Contemporary Islamic Movement," *International Insight,* p. 23.

36. Ottaway, David B., "Saudi King Backs Islamic Law Review," *The Washington Post,* June 16, 1983. *Ijtihad,* the principle of Islamic law which allows modification of existing interpretations of the law based on re-examination of original authoritative sources, was outlawed in the Tenth Century, A.D.

37. Algosaibi, "The New Arab World," in *Arabian Essays,* p. 115.

Chapter 1

1. Stewart, Desmond, *The Arab World,* pp. 9-10.

2. Dr. Levon H. Melikian (see bibliography) has studied the

modal personality of some Arab students, searching for traits to define "national character."

The author administered a word-association test to a group of Lebanese university students in 1972. The most common responses associated with the word "Arabs" were "generous," "brave," "honorable" and "loyal." About half of the forty-three respondents added the word "misunderstood."

3. This subject is very thoroughly discussed by Abdel-Rahim Omran in his book, *Population in the Arab World,* in the chapter, "The Contribution of the Arabs to World Culture and Science," pp. 13-41.

4. Slade, Shelley, "The Image of the Arab in America: Analysis of a Poll of American Attitudes," *Middle East Journal,* p. 143. Many of the stereotypes about the Middle East which are taught in schools or depicted in American media are discussed in *The Middle East, The Image and Reality,* edited by Jonathan Friedlander (see bibliography).

5. Nasir, Sari J., *The Arabs and the English,* p. 171.

Chapter 2

1. Patai, Raphael, *The Arab Mind,* pp. 60, 64, 65.
2. Hamady, Sania, *Temperament and Character of the Arabs,* p. 99.

Chapter 3

1. Atiyeh, George N., ed., *Arab and American Cultures,* p. 179.
2. Lawrence, T.E., *Seven Pillars of Wisdom,* p. 24.

Chapter 4

1. Laffin, John, *Rhetoric and Reality, The Arab Mind Considered,* pp. 78-79.
2. Hall, Edward T., *The Hidden Dimension,* p. 15.
3. Barakat, Robert A., "Talking with Hands," *Time,* p. 65.

Chapter 5

1. Anderson, Norman, *Law Reform in the Muslim World*, p. 63.

Chapter 6

1. Yousef, Fathi, "Cross-Cultural Communication Aspects of Contrastive Behavior Patterns between North Americans and Middle Easterners," *Human Organization*, p. 386.

2. Salah, Said, *Spoken Arabic*, p. 4.

3. Condon, John C. and Yousef, Fathi S.," The Middle Eastern Home," in *An Introduction to Intercultural Communication*, p. 160.

Chapter 8

1. Nyrop, Richard, ed., *Syria, A Country Study*, p. 30.

2. Thomas, Anthony and Deakin, Michael, *The Arab Experience*, p. 99.

3. Hall, Edward T., *The Hidden Dimension*, p. 5.

4. Anderson, Norman, *Law Reform in the Muslim World*, pp. 63, 69, 109, 114.

5. *Ibid.*, p. 116.

6. Sharabi, Hisham and Ani, Mukhtar, "Impact of Class and Culture on Social Behavior: The Feudal-Bourgeois Family in Arab Society," in *Psychological Dimensions of Near Eastern Studies*, edited by L. Carl Brown and Norman Itzkowitz, p. 248.

7. See, for example, the description of child-rearing practices in Sharabi and Ani's "Impact of Class and Culture on Social Behavior," cited above, or almost anywhere in Hamady's *Temperament and Character of the Arabs*.

8. Hamady, Sania, *Temperament and Character of the Arabs*, p. 32.

Chapter 9

1. A list of Koranic chapters in chronological order may be found in Richard Bell's *Introduction to the Qur'an*, (Edinburgh: University Press, 1953). The translation of the Koran by N.J. Dawood also presents the chapters in chronological rather than traditional order (N.J. Dawood, *The Koran*, New York: Penguin Books, 1964).

Chapter 10

1. The ten most widely spoken languages are:

Language	*Millions of Speakers*
Mandarin Chinese	720
English	305
Spanish	240
Arabic	150
Bengali	150
Russian	145
Portuguese	140
Hindi with Urdu	140
Japanese	120
German	105

From *Webster's Ninth New Collegiate Dictionary*. Springfield, Massachusetts: Merriam-Webster, Inc., 1983, p. 673.

2. A study was conducted in Tunisia in the early 70's, comparing the vocabulary of 6-year-old Tunsian children with equivalent vocabulary in Modern Standard Arabic, the medium through which they would be taught to read. It was found that over 70% of the vocabulary words were different. (Information from personal communication with professors, University of Tunis.)

3. McLoughlin, Leslie J., *Colloquial Arabic (Levantine)*, pp. 2-3.

Appendix A

1. The term "Levantine" is derived from the French name for the area bordering the eastern Mediterranean. This area (especially Lebanon and Syria) is referred to as "the Levant" in French and English.

2. Mandaville, Jon, "Impressions from a Writer's Notebook—At Home in Yemen," *Aramco World*, p. 30.

Appendix B

1. Nelson, Harold D., ed., *Morocco, A Country Study,* 4th edition. Washington, D.C.: American University Handbook Program, 1978, p. 49.

2. *Ibid.,* p. 125.

3. Lawson, Don, *Morocco, Algeria, Tunisia, and Libya*. New York: Franklin Watts, 1978, p. 9.

154

4. Nelson, Harold D., ed., *Tunisia, A Country Study,* 1st edition. Washington, D.C.: American University Handbook Program, 1979, p. 74.

5. Stone, Russell, ed., *Changes in Tunisia: Studies in the Social Sciences.* Albany: State University of New York Press, 1976, p. 164.

6. *Ibid.,* p. 165.

7. Allen, J.A., *Libya: The Experience of Oil.* Boulder: Westview Press, 1981, p. 22.

8. Lawson, *Morocco, Algeria, Tunisia, and Libya,* p. 49.

9. Deeb, Marius K. and Deeb, Mary Jane, *Libya Since the Revolution.* New York: Praeger Publisher, 1982, p. 59.

10. *Ibid.,* p. 65.

11. Nyrop, Richard F., ed, *Egypt, A Country Study,* 4th edition. Washington, D.C.: American University Handbook Program, 1983, p. 61.

12. *Ibid.,* p. 73.

13. *Ibid.,* p. 69.

14. *Ibid.,* p. 97.

15. Nelson, Harold D., ed., *Sudan, A Country Study,* 3rd edition. Washington, D.C.: American University Handbook Program, 1983, p. 84.

16. *Encyclopaedia Britannica,* 15th edition. Chicago: Encyclopaedia Brittanica, Inc., 1984. Volume 17, p. 763.

17. Gordon, David C., *The Republic of Lebanon: Nation in Jeopardy.* Boulder: Westview Press, 1983, p. 9.

18. *Ibid.,* p. 110.

19. Sinai, Anne and Pollack, Allen, eds., *The Syrian Arab Republic, A Handbook.* New York: American Association for Peace in the Middle East 1976, pp. 62-70.

20. *Encyclopaedia Brittanica,* Volume 17, p. 925.

21. Nyrop, Richard F., ed., *Jordan, A Country Study,* 3rd edition. Washington, D.C.: American University Handbook Program, 1980, p. 64.

22. *Ibid.,* p. 112.

23. *Encyclopaedia Brittanica,* Volume 9, p. 876.

24. Niblock, Tim, "Introduction," in *Social and Economic Development in the Arab Gulf,* edited by Tim Niblock. New York: St. Martin's Press, 1980, p. 83.

25. Cole, Donald P., "Pastoral Nomads in a Rapidly Changing Economy: The Case of Saudi Arabia," in *Social and Economic Development of the Arab Gulf*, p. 117.

26. Nyrop, Richard F., ed., *Saudi Arabia, A Country Study*, 3rd edition. Washington D.C.: American University Handbook Program, 1977, p. 45.

27. Palmer, Monte; Alghofaily, Ibrahim Fahad, and Alnimir, Saud Mohamed, "The Behavioral Correlates of Rentier Economics, A Case Study of Saudi Arabia," in *The Arabian Peninsula, Zone of Ferment*, edited by Robert W. Stookey. Stanford: Hoover Institute Press, 1984, p. 17.

28. Mansfield, Peter, *The New Arabians*. New York: Doubleday & Co., 1981, p. 184.

29. Stookey, Robert, *South Yemen: A Marxist Republic*. Boulder: Westview Press, 1982, p. 67.

30. Nyrop, Richard F., ed., *Area Handbook for the Yemens*, 1st edition. Washington, D.C.: American University Handbook Program, 1977, p. 71.

31. Stookey, *South Yemen: A Marxist Republic*, p. 88.

32. Niblock, "Introduction," p. 14.

33. Mansfield, *The New Arabians*, p. 112.

34. *Ibid.*, p. 116.

35. Birks, J.S., and Sinclair, C.A., "Economic and Social Implications of Current Development in the Arab Gulf: The Oriental Connection," in *Social and Economic Development in the Arab Gulf*, p. 139.

36. Lanier, Alison R., *Update: Bahrain and Qatar*. Chicago: Intercultural Press, Inc., 1978, p. 8.

37. Khuri, Fuad I., *Tribe and State in Bahrain: The Transformation of Social and Political Authority in an Arab State*. Chicago: University of Chicago Press, 1980, p. 130.

38. Birks and Sinclair, "Economic and Social Implications of Current Development in the Arab Gulf: The Oriental Connection," p. 139.

39. Melikian, Levon H., *Jassim: A Study in the Psychological Development of a Young Man in Qatar*. London: Longman Group Ltd., 1981, p. 52.

40. *Ibid.*, p. 34.

41. Niblock, "Introduction," p. 13.

42. *Encyclopaedia Britannica,* Volume 13, p. 567.

43. Malone, J.J., "Involvement and Change: The Coming of the Oil Age to Saudi Arabia," in *Social and Economic Development in the Arab Gulf,* p. 18.

Bibliography and References

I. BOOKS

Abu-Sinna, Mohamed Ibrahim, *Falsafatu Al-Mathali Al-Sha'bi (The Philosophy of Folk Proverbs)*. Cairo: Ministry of Culture (Cultural Library Series No. 193), 1968.

Al-Ba'albaki, Munir, "English Words of Arabic Origin," in *Al-Mawrid, A Modern English-Arabic Dictionary*. Beirut: Dar El-Ilm Lil-Malayen, 1982, pp. 101-112.

Al-Farsy, Fouad, *Saudi Arabia—A Case Study in Development,* (Second edition). London: Stacey International, 1980.

Algosaibi, Ghazi A., *Arabian Essays*. London: Kegan Paul International Ltd., 1982.

Allan, J. A., *Libya: The Experience of Oil*. Boulder: Westview Press, 1981.

Almaney, A. J., and Alwan, A. J., *Communicating with the Arabs, A Handbook for the Business Executive*. Prospect Heights, Illinois: Waveland Press, Inc., 1982.

Al-Muhafaza, Ali, *Al-Ittijaahaat Al-Fikriyya 'ind Al-'Arab (Trends in Arab Thought)*. Beirut: Al-Ahliyya lil-Nashr wal-Tawzii', 1975.

Anderson, Norman, *Law Reform in the Muslim World*. London: University of London, The Athlone Press, 1976.

Arberry, A. J., *The Koran Interpreted*. New York: Macmillan, 1955.

Area Handbook for Lebanon, 2nd edition. Washington, D.C.: American University Handbook Program, 1974.

Atiyeh, George N., ed., *Arab and American Cultures.* Washington, D.C.: American Enterprise Institute for Public Policy Research, 1977.

Baer, Gabriel, *Studies in the Social History of Modern Egypt.* Chicago: University of Chicago Press, 1969.

Beck, Lois, and Keddie, Nikki, eds., *Women in the Muslim World.* Cambridge: Harvard University Press, 1978.

Berque, Jacques, *Cultural Expression in Arab Society Today.* Austin: University of Texas Press, 1978.

Bezergan, Najm, "Language and Reality in the Arab World," in *The Arabs Today: Alternatives for Tomorrow,* edited by Edward Said and Fuad Suleiman. Columbus, Ohio: Forum Associates, Inc., 1973, pp. 23-30.

Birks, J. S., and Sinclair, C. A., "Economic and Social Implications of Current Development in the Arab Gulf: The Oriental Connection," in *Social and Economic Development in the Arab Gulf,* edited by Tim Niblock. New York: St. Martin's Press, 1980, pp. 135-150.

Carmichael, Joel, *Arabs Today.* New York: Anchor Press/Doubleday, 1977.

Cole, Donald P., "Pastoral Nomads in a Rapidly Changing Economy: The Case of Saudi Arabia," in *Social and Economic Development in the Arab Gulf,* edited by Tim Niblock. New York: St. Martin's Press, 1980, pp. 106-121.

Condon, John, and Yousef, Fathi S., "The Middle Eastern Home," in *An Introduction to Intercultural Communication.* Indianapolis: The Bobbs-Merrill Co., Inc., 1977, pp. 159-162.

Deeb, Marius K., and Deeb, Mary Jane, *Libya Since the Revolution.* New York: Praeger Publishers, 1982.

Encyclopaedia Britannica, 15th edition. Chicago: Encyclopaedia Britannica Inc., 1984.

Fernea, Elizabeth Warnock, and Bezirgan, Basima Qattan, eds., *Middle Eastern Muslim Women Speak.* Austin: University of Texas Press, 1977.

Friedlander, Jonathan, ed., *The Middle East: The Image and the Reality.* Los Angeles: University of California (Curriculum Inquiry Center) Press, 1981.

Gordon, David C., *The Republic of Lebanon: Nation in Jeopardy.* Boulder: Westview Press, 1983.

Hall, Edward T., *The Hidden Dimension.* New York: Doubleday & Co., Inc., 1966.

Hamady, Sania, *Temperament and Character of the Arabs.* New York: Twayne, 1960.

Husain, S.S., and Ashraf, S.A., eds., *Crisis in Muslim Education.* Jeddah: King Abdulaziz University, 1979.

Jureidini, Paul A., and McLaurin, R.D., *Jordan, The Impact of Social Change on the Role of the Tribes.* Washington, D.C.: Praeger Publishers, 1984.

Khouja, M.W., and Sadler, P.G., *The Economy of Kuwait—Development and Role in International Finance.* London: The Macmillan Press Ltd., 1979.

Khuri, Fuad I., *Tribe and State in Bahrain: The Transformation of Social and Political Authority in an Arab State.* Chicago: University of Chicago Press, 1980.

Kingdom of Saudi Arabia Statistical Yearbook, (Seventeenth issue). Riyadh: Central Department of Statistics, 1981.

Laffin, John, *Rhetoric and Reality, The Arab Mind Considered.* New York: Taplinger Publishing Co., 1975.

Lanier, Alison R., *Update: Bahrain and Qatar.* Chicago: Intercultural Press, Inc., 1978.

———, *Update: Egypt.* Chicago: Intercultural Press, Inc., 1982.

———, *Update: Saudi Arabia.* Chicago: Intercultural Press, Inc., 1981.

———, *Update: United Arab Emirates.* Chicago: Intercultural Press, Inc., 1978.

Laroui, Abdallah, *Crisis of the Arab Intellectual.* Berkeley: University of California Press, 1976.

Lawrence, T.E., *Seven Pillars of Wisdom.* New York: Doubleday & Co., Inc., 1926.

Lawson, Don, *Morocco, Algeria, Tunisia, and Libya.* New York: Franklin Watts, 1978.

Lee, Eve, *The American in Saudi Arabia.* Chicago: Intercultural Press, Inc., 1980.

Lewis, Bernard, ed., *Islam and the Arab World.* New York: Knopf, 1976.

Lutfiyya, Abdulla M., and Churchill, Charles W., eds., *Readings in Arab Middle Eastern Societies and Cultures*. The Hague: Mouton, 1970.

Malone, J.J., "Involvement and Change: The Coming of the Oil Age to Saudi Arabia," in *Social and Economic Development in the Arab Gulf,* edited by Tim Niblock. New York: St. Martin's Press, 1980, pp. 49-60.

Mansfield, Peter, *The New Arabians*. New York: Doubleday & Co., 1981.

McLoughlin, Leslie J., *Colloquial Arabic (Levantine)*. London: Routledge & Kegan Paul Ltd., 1982.

Melikian, Levon H., *Jassim: A Study in the Psychological Development of a Young Man in Qatar*. London: Longman Group Ltd., 1981.

_____, "The Modal Personality of Saudi College Students: A Study in National Character," in *Psychological Dimensions of Near Eastern Studies,* edited by L. Carl Brown and Norman Itzkowitz. Princeton: The Darwin Press, 1977, pp. 166-209.

The Middle East and North Africa 1979-80, Twenty-sixth edition. London: Europa Publications Ltd., 1979.

Nasir, Sari J., *The Arabs and the English,* Second edition. London: Longman Group Ltd., 1979.

Nawwab, Ismail I.; Speers, Peter C.; and Hoye, Paul F., eds., *Aramco and Its World*. Washington, D.C.: Arabian American Oil Co., 1980.

Nelson, Harold D., ed., *Algeria, A Country Study,* 3rd edition. Washington, D.C.: American University Handbook Program, 1979.

_____, *Morocco, A Country Study,* 4th edition. Washington, D.C.: American University Handbook Program, 1978.

_____, *Sudan, A Country Study,* 3rd edition. Washington, D.C.: American University Handbook Program, 1983.

_____, *Tunisia, A Country Study,* 1st edition. Washington, D.C.: American University Handbook Program, 1979.

Niblock, Tim, "Introduction," in *Social and Economic Development in the Arab Gulf,* edited by Tim Niblock. New York: St. Martin's Press, 1980, pp. 11-19.

Nyrop, Richard F., ed., *Area Handbook for the Persian Gulf States,* 1st edition. Washington, D.C.: American University Handbook Program, 1977.

_____, *Area Handbook for the Yemens,* 1st edition. Washington, D.C.: American University Handbook Program, 1977.

_____, *Egypt, A Country Study,* 4th edition. Washington, D.C.: American University Handbook Program, 1983.

_____, *Iraq, A Country Study,* 3rd edition. Washington, D.C.: American University Handbook Program, 1979.

_____, *Jordan, A Country Study,* 3rd edition. Washington, D.C.: American University Handbook Program, 1980.

_____, *Saudi Arabia, A Country Study,* 3rd edition. Washington, D.C.: American University Handbook Program, 1977.

_____, *Syria, A Country Study,* 3rd edition. Washington, D.C.: American University Handbook Program, 1979.

Omran, Abdel-Rahim, *Population in the Arab World.* London: Croom Helm Ltd., 1980.

Palmer, Monte; Alghofaily, Ibrahim Fahad, and Alnimir, Saud Mohamed, "The Behavioral Correlates of Rentier Economics, A Case Study of Saudi Arabia," in *The Arabian Peninsula, Zone of Ferment,* edited by Robert W. Stookey. Stanford: Hoover Institution Press, 1984, pp. 17-36.

Parssinen, Catherine, "The Changing Role of Women," in *King Faisal and the Modernisation of Saudi Arabia,* edited by Willard A. Beling. London: Croom Helm Ltd., 1980, pp. 145-170.

Patai, Raphael, *The Arab Mind.* New York: Scribner, 1973.

_____, *Golden River to Golden Road.* Philadelphia: University of Pennsylvania Press, 1962.

Peterson, J.E., *Oman in the Twentieth Century, Political Foundations of an Emerging State.* New York: Barnes & Noble Books, 1978.

_____, *Yemen: The Search for a Modern State.* Baltimore: Johns Hopkins University Press, 1982.

Prothro, Edwin T., *Child Rearing in the Lebanon.* Cambridge: Harvard University Press, 1961.

Qutb, Muhammad, "The Role of Religion in Education," in *Aims and Objectives of Islamic Education,* edited by S.N. Al-Attas. Jeddah: King Abdulaziz University, 1979, pp. 48-62.

Raban, Jonathan, *Arabia: A Journey through the Labyrinth.* New York: Simon & Schuster, 1979.

El-Rashidi, Galal, *The Arabs and the World of the Seventies.* New Delhi: Vikas Publishing House Ltd., 1977.

El-Sadat, Anwar, *In Search of Identity*. New York: Harper & Row, 1977.

Salah, Said, *Spoken Arabic*. Dhahran: I.P.A., 1982.

Samovar, Larry A.; Richard E. Porter; and Nemi C. Jain, *Understanding Intercultural Communication*. Belmont, Calif.: Wadsworth Publishing Co., 1981.

Sardar, Ziauddin, *Science, Technology, and Development in the Muslim World*. Atlantic Highlands, N.J.: Humanities Press, 1977.

Schilling, Nancy A., *Doing Business in Saudi Arabia and the Arab Gulf States*. New York: Inter-Crescent Publishing and Information Corp., 1975.

Sharabi, Hisham, and Mukhtar Ani, "Impact of Class and Culture on Social Behavior: The Feudal-Bourgeois Family in Arab Society," in *Psychological Dimensions of Near Eastern Studies,* edited by L. Carl Brown and Norman Itzkowitz. Princeton: The Darwin Press, 1977, pp. 240-256.

Sinai, Anne, and Allen Pollack eds., *The Syrian Arab Republic, A Handbook*. New York: American Association for Peace in the Middle East, 1976.

Stewart, Desmond, *The Arab World*. New York: Time-Life Books, 1972.

Stone, Russell, ed., *Changes in Tunisia: Studies in the Social Sciences*. Albany: State University of New York Press, 1976.

Stookey, Robert W., ed., *The Arabian Peninsula, Zone of Ferment*. Stanford: Hoover Institution Press, 1984.

———, *South Yemen: A Marxist Republic*. Boulder: Westview Press, 1982.

Thomas, Anthony, and Michael Deakin, *The Arab Experience*. London: Namara Publications Ltd., 1975.

Wehr, Hans, "Introduction," in *A Dictionary of Modern Written Arabic,* edited by J. Milton Cowan. Beirut: Librairie du Liban, 1980, pp. vii-xii.

Wells, Donald A., *Saudi Arabia Development Strategy*. Washington, D.C.: American Enterprise Institute for Public Policy Research, 1976.

Winstone, H.V.F., and Freeth, Zahra, *Kuwait, Prospect and Reality*. New York: Crane, Russak & Co., Inc., 1972.

Zahlan, A.B., "The Social Responsibility of the Arab Scientist," in *The Arabs Today: Alternatives for Tomorrow,* edited by Edward

Said and Fuad Suleiman. Columbus, Ohio: Forum Associates, Inc., 1973, pp. 43-58.

Zahlan, Rosemarie Said, *The Creation of Qatar*. Totowa, N.J.: Barnes & Noble, 1979.

II. ARTICLES

Antoun, Richard T., "On the Significance of Names in an Arab Village," *Ethnology*, Vol. VII, No. 2, April 1968, pp. 158-170.

Barakat, Robert A., "Talking with Hands," *Time*, September 17, 1973, pp. 65-66.

Eilts, Helen Brew, "Women in Modern Egypt," *International Insight*, Vol. I, No. 6, July/August 1981, pp. 25-28.

El Guindi, Fadwa, "Is There an Islamic Alternative? The Case of Egypt's Contemporary Islamic Movement," *International Insight*, Vol. I, No. 6, July/August 1981, pp. 19-24.

Gulick, John, ed., "Dimensions of Cultural Change in the Middle East," (Special Issue), *Human Organization*, Vol. 24, No. 1, Spring 1965.

Haim, Sylvia G., "The Situation of the Arab Woman in the Mirror of Literature," *Middle Eastern Studies*, Vol. 17, No. 4, October 1981, pp. 510-30.

Hall, Edward T., "Learning the Arabs' Silent Language," *Psychology Today*, Vol. 13, No. 3, August 1979, pp. 45-54.

Hamalian, Leo, "Communication by Gesture in the Middle East," *Etc.*, Vol. 22, No. 1, March 1965, pp. 43-49.

Hottinger, Arnold, "The Depth of Arab Radicalism," *Foreign Affairs*, Vol. 5, No. 3, April 1973, pp. 491-504.

Iseman, Peter A., "The Arabian Ethos," *Harper's*, Vol. 256, No. 1533, February 1978, pp. 37-56.

Mandaville, Jon, "Impressions from a Writer's Notebook—At Home in Yemen," *Aramco World*, Vol. 32, No. 3, May/June 1981, pp. 30-33.

Morris, Claud, "The Media and the Ugly Arab," *World Press Review*, Vol. 27, No. 8, August 1980, p. 57.

"Oman: An Introduction," *Aramco World*, Vol, 34, No. 3, May/June 1983, p. 2.

Ottaway, David B., "Saudi King Backs Islamic Law Review," *The Washington Post*, June 16, 1983.

Shouby, E., "The Influence of the Arabic Language on the Psychology of the Arabs," *Middle East Journal*, Vol. 5, No. 3, Summer 1951, pp. 284-302.

Slade, Shelley, "The Image of the Arab in America: Analysis of a Poll of American Attitudes," *Middle East Journal*, Vol. 35, No. 2, Spring 1981, pp. 143-162.

Willis, David K., "The Impact of Islam," *The Christian Science Monitor* (Weekly International Edition), August 18-24, 1984.

_____, "The Practice of Islam," *The Christian Science Monitor* (Weekly International Edition), July 28-August 3, 1984.

Wright, Edwin M., "The Interrelationship of the Religions of the Middle East—Judaism, Christianity and Islam," *International Insight*, Vol. I, Number V, May/June 1981, pp. 37-39.

Yousef, Fathi S., "Cross-Cultural Communication Aspects of Contrastive Behavior Patterns between North Americans and Middle Easterners," *Human Organization*, Vol. 33, No. 4, Winter 1974, pp. 383-87.

"1.1 Billion Being Spent on Girls' Schools," *Arab News*, September 13, 1983.